About This Book

Why is this topic important?

When we consider how learning is accomplished most effectively, we recognize that it is goal-oriented, contextual, interesting, challenging, and interactive. These characteristics also define computer games, from which we can infer that the most effective learning experience is also an engaging one. That is, learning *should* be hard fun. However, if that is our goal, we also need to know *how* to design such experiences.

What can you achieve with this book?

The book presents a research-based and experience-grounded framework for systematically aligning the elements of learning and engagement and provides an associated design process. With this support, a reader can take any learning objective and work it through to an engaging learning experience. The book includes tools to assist the learner in systematically transforming learning from humdrum to fun.

How is this book organized?

The book starts out by presenting the elements of learning and the elements of engagement. It shows how the two can be aligned, thus creating a unified set of elements to be achieved. It then characterizes a suite of approaches that provide various pragmatic approaches from an enhanced instructional design to a full game engine. Subsequently, it develops a design process that discusses how to mix engagement with learning. The book discusses pragmatic issues in implementation, as well as directions for the future.

About Pfeiffer

Pfeiffer serves the professional development and hands-on resource needs of training and human resource practitioners and gives them products to do their jobs better. We deliver proven ideas and solutions from experts in HR development and HR management, and we offer effective and customizable tools to improve workplace performance. From novice to seasoned professional, Pfeiffer is the source you can trust to make yourself and your organization more successful.

Essential Knowledge Pfeiffer produces insightful, practical, and comprehensive materials on topics that matter the most to training and HR professionals. Our Essential Knowledge resources translate the expertise of seasoned professionals into practical, how-to guidance on critical workplace issues and problems. These resources are supported by case studies, worksheets, and job aids and are frequently supplemented with CD-ROMs, Web sites, and other means of making the content easier to read, understand, and use.

Essential Tools Pfeiffer's Essential Tools resources save time and expense by offering proven, ready-to-use materials—including exercises, activities, games, instruments, and assessments—for use during a training or team-learning event. These resources are frequently offered in looseleaf or CD-ROM format to facilitate copying and customization of the material.

Pfeiffer also recognizes the remarkable power of new technologies in expanding the reach and effectiveness of training. While e-hype has often created whizbang solutions in search of a problem, we are dedicated to bringing convenience and enhancements to proven training solutions. All our e-tools comply with rigorous functionality standards. The most appropriate technology wrapped around essential content yields the perfect solution for today's on-the-go trainers and human resource professionals.

Essential resources for training and HR professionals

Engaging Learning

Designing e-Learning Simulation Games

CLARK N. QUINN

Pfeiffer
A Wiley Imprint
www.pfeiffer.com

Published by Pfeiffer
An Imprint of Wiley
989 Market Street, San Francisco, CA 94103-1741
www.pfeiffer.com

Readers should be aware that Internet Web sites offered as citations and/or sources for further information may have changed or disappeared between the time this was written and when it is read.

For additional copies/bulk purchases of this book in the U.S. please contact 800-274-4434.

Pfeiffer books and products are available through most bookstores. To contact Pfeiffer directly call our Customer Care Department within the U.S. at 800-274-4434, outside the U.S. at 317-572-3985, fax 317-572-4002, or visit www.pfeiffer.com.

Pfeiffer also publishes its books in a variety of electronic formats. Some content that appears in print may not be available in electronic books.

ISBN: 0-7879-7522-2

Library of Congress Cataloging-in-Publication Data

Quinn, Clark N., date.
    Engaging learning: designing e-learning simulation games/Clark N.
Quinn, Marcia L Connor.
        p. cm.
    Includes bibliographical references and index.
    ISBN 0-7879-7522-2 (alk. paper)
    1. Simulation games in education—Design and construction.
2. Computer-assisted instruction. I. Connor, Marcia L. II. Title.
    LB1029.S53.Q85 2005
    371.39'7—dc22

                                                    2005001852

Acquiring Editor: Lisa Shannon   Manufacturing Supervisor: Becky Carreño
Director of Development: Kathleen Dolan Davies Editorial Assistant: Laura Reizman
Production Editor: Nina Kreiden   Illustrations: Lotus Art
Editor: Suzanne Copenhagen

Printed in the United States of America

Printing   10 9 8 7 6 5 4 3

To the next generation, who make all this important, and specifically to my children, **DECLAN** and **ERIN**, who have taught me much about wonder and the joy of learning. May all your learning be fun and lead to great success.

CONTENTS

Foreword   xv

Preface   xix

Acknowledgments   xxiii

Introduction   1

    Audience   1

    Product Description   2

    Related Products   2

    Explanation of Model or Theory   2

    Glossary of Key Terms   3

    Facilitator's Guidelines   4

PART A

Setting the Stage

Chapter 1: Games? Really?   9

   Engaging Experiences   11

   Why Engagement?   13

   The Learning-Doing Continuum   15

   The Payoff   17

   Road Map   18

Chapter 2: Learning Basics   23

   Instructional Design   24

   Cognitive Enhancements   29

   A Convergent Model   33

   Summary   37

Chapter 3: Experience Basics   39

   Engagement   40

   Sources   43

   Synthesis   48

   Summary   49

PART B

A Play in Three Acts

Chapter 4: Engagement-Education Synergy   53

Implications 55

Summary 64

Case Study 1: "Quest for Independence" 64

Chapter 5: Trajectory 75

Level 1: Mini-Scenarios 77

Case Study 2: "MediaSpeak" 80

Level 2: Linked Scenarios 87

Case Study 3: Project Management Overview, Phase 1 89

Level 3: Contingent Scenarios 95

Case Study 4: Vehicle Selling 96

Level 4: The Full Monty 102

Case Study 5: Drug Therapy Demo 107

Trade-offs 112

Chapter 6: A Design Process 113

Design Basics 114

Design Stages 116

Instructional Design 123

Engagement Perspective 125

Engaged Design: Creating Meaningful Practice 128

Engaged Design: The Process 132

Summary 153

Summary Checklist 153

PART C

Set Design and Afterthoughts

Chapter 7: Pragmatics   157

    Budget   157

    Production   159

    Prototyping Tools   160

    Media   162

    Writing   165

    Humor   166

    Cartoons and Comics   166

    Culture   167

    Gender   169

    Age and Development   169

    Evaluation   170

    Multiplayer Games   171

    Nonelectronic Games and Electronic Interactions   172

    Technology Environments   173

    Teams and Talent   175

Chapter 8: Future Issues   179

    Affect   179

    Learning Objects   180

    Going Mobile   182

    Personalization   183

    Meta-Learning   184

New Input and Output Technologies   185

Design Magic   186

Chapter 9: Conclusion   187

Where We've Been   188

Just Do It   189

When to Do It   191

Where to Go for Further Information   192

Tally Ho!   194

Bibliography   195

Index   201

About the Author   209

LEARNING IS A UNIVERSAL experience; it is the primary force that allows humans and animals alike to survive—and thrive—in their environment. So why is the practice of learning so different across cultures, age groups, and subjects? Why, specifically, is learning closely associated with anxiety, frustration, and boredom by so many people across the world? Why does learning frighten us when it can so easily be accomplished by even the youngest of babies and the grizzliest of bears, who seem to get great pleasure with every new discovery and, as a result, adapt and adopt seemingly nonstop?

There might be a simple explanation for this seeming contradiction. Many of us have been taught that to be valuable, education must be made serious, quantifiable, and disassociated from fun, activity, and the ongoing nature of daily living. It is often relegated to the status of a time-consuming burden rather than considered one of life's true joys. I believe that learning can and should be a rewarding process that reveals new opportunities to learn even more. Curiosity, play, and engagement are the key ingredients—along with an understanding and a belief that learning is a natural practice that we were born to pursue. This perspective applies to more than informal or ad hoc over-the-water-cooler learning.

I know firsthand that formal education programs, including those driven by technology, can truly become effective and meaningful when they employ compelling activity-based approaches such as games and simulations. I've come to that conclusion after spending many years creating global education organizations, researching then writing about how learning influences life across the lifespan, and working directly with thousands of learners of all ages in many different settings.

When you involve learners in compelling ways you unleash their intrinsic capacity to make cognitive leaps and build on what they already know. After all, learning does not occur only between the ears; brain and body operate as a single entity, so the more of themselves learners use, the more likely they are to learn quickly, comfortably, easily, and efficiently. Furthermore, games and simulations help us play with limitless possibilities, have fun, and explore without suffering serious consequences. In a game you constantly improvise and invent new responses, adjust your approach, and try again while you are still interested so that you can improve and polish your techniques.

How ironic that some hardened business leaders and administrators look down their noses at these benefits, demanding narrowly defined results and questioning the resources dedicated to creating appealing experiences because they seem too interesting to be valuable. I encourage you not to let their grousing slow you down. Don't waste another day creating programs where the only thing played with is the learner's attention span. Help bring the joy of learning into everything you do and make a real difference in the lives of people turning to you for guidance.

Engaging Learning: Designing e-Learning Simulation Games can show you how. I first met Clark Quinn almost a decade ago when I was looking to learn from the best, and I'm thrilled that he has finally taken the time to write this down. I believe you will find that the book you are holding is equally useful for the curious learner as for the e-learning developer interested in creating something truly special. It explains beautifully and gently not only how to craft more meaningful learning experiences, but also why it is vital to do so. I look forward to seeing what you create as a result of what you learn here— you have the opportunity to truly change the world.

March 2005   *Marcia L. Conner*
                                                          Ageless Learner
                                                          Staunton, Virginia

HOW DID I END UP HERE? It's a bit of a story. . . . After changing my major several times in college, I ended up choosing computer science. I was also tutoring (calculus, physics, and chemistry) for some extra pocket money. I managed to get a job with Carmel Myers and Ken Majer doing the computer support for the campus office that ran the tutoring. A light went on, and I realized that computers to support learning could be a valuable and fascinating task. It helps to know that at the time, the major occupation for computer graduates in Southern California, where I was born and raised and went to school, was to write missile guidance programs. As a product of my times, this did not appeal to me, but I had just found the perfect calling: I could help people achieve their personal goals and improve themselves, and I could play with cool toys!

My college had no such program (few did at the time), but it did allow me to create my own major. I looked around campus and found that Jim Levin and Hugh Mehan were pioneering this work, and they agreed to serve as advisors. I was off and running, assisting their project on using e-mail as an alternate channel for classroom discussion (this was in 1979).

After college, I called all over the country trying to find someone who wanted to hire me in the area of computer-based education. After a long time, someone pointed me to Jim Schuyler, who was correctly reputed to have his finger on the pulse. I called and asked him whom I might call to find a job doing computers and learning. He had just formed a company doing computer games for publishers to accompany textbooks, and my career was launched. I had a grand couple of years making computers sing and dance, but I got frustrated that we were doing such low-level games. We experimented a lot with other games (Jim once gave each member of the team a roll of quarters and we all went to the arcade to try out new video games). After experiencing my first adventure game (the classic "Colossal Cave"), I was hooked. I recognized that such a game had great learning potential, and Jim agreed, but he was concerned that it was not commercially viable.

In my undergraduate program, I had been exposed to artificial intelligence and was a bit of an AI groupie. A friend and I met every month or so for lunch and to chat about it. That was my entrée to cognitive science, so I was primed when I read an article calling for "cognitive engineering"—applying what was known about how people think and learn as the basis for designing systems. I had been wrestling with how we should design our game interfaces, and I knew that this was what I wanted to go to graduate school to study.

The author of the article was Donald Norman, and I contacted him to ask where I could study cognitive engineering. He graciously met with me, and even more graciously invited me to study with him. Thus began a Ph.D. in applied cognitive science. After a false start or two, my thesis ended up being about analogical reasoning and how it might be improved. I had become interested in meta-cognition, thinking about your own thinking, and focusing on general thinking skills was a theme that has remained throughout my work. Don has remained not only an intellectual inspiration, but also a willing supporter.

I managed to secure a postdoctoral fellowship at the University of Pittsburgh's Learning Research and Development Center, and while ostensibly working on supporting children's mental models of science, I created a game that optimally required analogical reasoning to succeed. That game bug just wouldn't stop biting me.

After my postdoc, I obtained an academic position at the University of New South Wales in Australia. As an academic I was free to pursue my own research agenda, and I started to systematically evaluate the elements that led to learning. While there, my background in games led me to be asked to create a game to assist children growing up without parents to learn to live independently. I was blessed in that although I had no resources, a talented student was looking for a meaningful project. Working together, Dana Kedziar and I developed a game that was well received. Buoyed by that experience, I conducted a variety of research projects with interested students, which spurred on my work. It was then that I began to formulate the framework that has resulted in this book.

I began to feel frustrated that my own university was not investing in learning technology. Also, I recognized that some experience in management would benefit me. I took a leave of absence when the opportunity to work with a government-sponsored initiative in online learning arose. I moved from that project to another, where I gained the opportunity to develop some online content. Working with a talented multimedia producer, Jan Zwar, I had the challenge of creating compelling and effective learning content. We allowed creative tension to drive an engaging product with several innovations (though stopping well short of a full game). This taste of commercial pragmatics and rigor was quite useful.

After the birth of our first child, my wife and I felt our homing instinct kicking in, and I started looking into returning to the United States. Jim Schuyler had just joined a new learning initiative and contacted me. He ended up bringing me back to the United States to lead a project for the company he worked for. The CEO of the organization was Joe Miller. Although the project was not about games (I do other e-learning things, too), Joe had headed game development at Sega, and I took the opportunity to pick his brain about the realities of the game industry.

That engagement ended rather abruptly (as did many other things in the spring of 2001), and I needed another way to earn a living. I eventually found my living consulting on e-learning, often focused specifically on making better e-learning. This has included a number of game projects. I realized that as an industry the e-learning field is woefully underachieving, and I have an approach that can help. It was time to get this book out to help improve the quality of the learning experience.

And here we are.

ACKNOWLEDGMENTS

THERE ARE FAR more contributors to my understanding of games and learning, and to my ability to complete this book, than I will ever be able to list. That said, there are some I absolutely must acknowledge. As many others have disclaimed, those I mention deserve credit for all that's right here and none of the blame for any faults, which is mine alone to shoulder. Thanks to all of you!

I've been fortunate in my career to have many mentors who have helped me. The individuals mentioned by name in the preface have served as mentors: Carmel Myers, Ken Majer, Jim Levin, Hugh Mehan, Don Norman, and Joe Miller. Jim Schuyler in particular has been mentor, colleague, and friend. Paul Compton, Ron Watts, and Rim Keris have served as sources of knowledge and models for behavior. Further back, my AP English teacher, Richard Bergeron, modeled what I later learned is an exemplary participatory and constructivist form of learning that helped me learn how to think.

I've benefited from several individuals who have allowed me the pleasure of working with them on game or gamelike projects: Charlie Gillette of Knowledge Anywhere, Jason Shaeffer (then at Vis-a-vis), and Mohit Bhargava of LearningMate.

I've had conversations with or have heard a number of people, including Will Wright, Eric Zimmerman, Kurt Squire, Judy Brown, and Henry Jenkins, on games (among other things), for which I'm grateful. I was greatly appreciative of the time Marc Prensky and Clark Aldrich, gurus of the corporate use of learning games, spent talking with me.

Many others have provided connections or opportunities, such as Shirley Alexander and Sandra Wills in Australia, Paul Brna in the UK, and Jim Spohrer and Marcia Conner in the United States, who are owed thanks more than I can possibly express. I must mention Bill Daul, through whom I met Jay Cross, Claudia Wells, and Claudia L'Amoreaux. Together we formed the Meta-Learning Lab, and their different perspectives on learning as well as their support have been of immense value. Jay has played a mentor role as well.

Jay Cross also served as a reviewer of the manuscript for this book, as did Godfrey Parkin, Mark Oehlert, and Brooke Broadbent. Their comments have massively improved the book, though of course they draw no responsibility, and consequently no blame, for any remaining errors.

Mention must be made of the folks at Pfeiffer, who have shepherded me through the process. Lisa Shannon, Laura Reizman, Kathleen Dolan Davies, Jessie Mandle, Suzanne Copenhagen, and Nina Kreiden have provided good feedback to keep me on track.

The final mention rightly goes to my family. My mother and father, Esther and Nives, have provided wonderful role models about who to be, how to be, and how important learning is. My extended family, including brother and in-laws and their families, have shown nothing but encouragement, for which I'm grateful. My wife, LeAnn, has been my muse, inspiring and supporting me as well as challenging me. She's also always my first and best editor. To her and our children goes the final mention: my grateful thanks and all my love.

Engaging
Learning

THE PURPOSE OF THIS BOOK is to present the reader with a process to design e-learning simulation games. Such learning experiences are needed to capitalize on e-learning. It turns out that the elements that make an experience engaging also are the ones that make it an effective learning experience. However, this alignment has not been understood, and without this understanding, efforts to team educators with media or game experts are not likely to succeed. There are too many design opportunities and too little understanding. This book is designed to address that gap.

Audience

The book is intended both for education folks who want to move beyond traditional e-learning to have a greater impact and for game industry or other non-education folks charged with creating a learning game. Both audiences could and should include corporate trainers, learning software designers, game teams, and so forth. The book is also intended to serve as a text to be used in courses on learning game design, which are increasingly seen in bachelor's and master's programs in educational technology and similar degrees. The principles described in this book are also applicable to the broader category of experience design, interaction design, and other ways to characterize designing interactive technology for individuals.

Product Description

The book provides overviews of the elements of learning and engagement, discusses the alignment of the two, presents several models of increasing complexity (and value) that approach full games, delineates a systematic design process, and provides coverage of both pragmatic and future issues. The book is illustrated with diagrams and examples and provides several tools to assist in the design process.

Related Products

A Web site accompanies the book to support adding new resources after the book's publication. See the URL www.engaginglearning.com.

Explanation of Model or Theory

The underlying model of the book is that the elements of learning and engagement can be aligned (see Table I-1) to create a synergy that can be exploited to systematically design compelling learning experiences. In Table I-1 we see that the list of elements from learning matches the elements from engagement, and we have created a list that integrates the two.

Table I-1. Element Alignment.

Learning Elements	Engagement Elements	Synergy
Contextualized	Thematic coherence	Theme
Clear goal	Clear goal	Goal
Appropriate challenge	Balanced challenge	Challenge
Anchored	Relevance: action to domain	Action-Domain link
Relevant	Relevance: problem to learner	Problem-Learner link
Exploratory	Choices of action	Active
Active manipulation	Direct manipulation	Direct
Appropriate feedback	Coupling	Feedback
Attention-getting	Novel information and events	Affect

Glossary of Key Terms

The key to developing engaging learning requires understanding the elements of engagement (and learning), ensuring that objectives are of a high-enough level to require the real application of knowledge to solve problems, capturing reliable misconceptions that are possessed by learners as alternatives to the correct answer, and then using these components to place the learner in a story-driven setting where they make decisions based on those objectives.

- *Engagement:* the situation of having attention fully focused on a particular task
- *Objective:* in the case of learning, a well-defined behavior that learners need to be able to perform

- *Misconception:* a reliable and repeatable mistake learners make in applying knowledge, based on an erroneous model

- *Decision:* a choice made meaningful by requiring knowledge applied in a context

Facilitator's Guidelines

There are several activities that naturally accompany this book. In general, for design processes, experiencing and critiquing other designs is a good way to internalize the underlying principles. Then the principles need to be exercised in some design tasks. Reciprocal teaching, whereby the instructor models critiquing and then the learners take turns practicing critiques, helps develop monitoring skills that, when internalized, become self-monitoring and then self-improving skills.

Consequently, the first category of activity for those who come from an *educational* background is to experience a variety of *engaging* experiences (or recall past ones) and then reflect on what made that experience engaging (or not). What are factors common across these experiences? This reflection can be done before reviewing the theory to initiate the development of ideas, and it definitely should be done after considering the theory to begin to apply the framework. The engaging experiences should include some subset of computer games, toys, particularly nice computer interfaces, movies, books, plays, and theater.

For those from an *engagement* background, we need to do the same for *educational* materials. Experience a variety of educational experiences (or recall past ones), and then reflect on what made that experience effective (or not). What are factors common across these experiences? As in the previous instance, this can be done before reviewing the theory to initiate the development of ideas, and it definitely should be done after considering the theory to begin to apply the framework. The educational experiences should include taking some subset of seminars, computer-based or Web-based courses, reading an encyclopedia entry or a book, watching a documentary, and listening to an audio course.

The second category of activity is to give learners an educational objective and have them design learning games. They should start by creating overarching story lines and then gradually go through more of the process. For instance, they might take an embryonic story line and then have to flesh it out. Ideally, their summative task would be to design a full game. A variation would be to let learners choose an objective (after the facilitator reviews the objective for appropriateness) and design an associated game. The objectives could get progressively more challenging.

The facilitator's role is to guide the discussion, help flesh out the principles in the first category of activity, and then help integrate the principles into a coherent design process.

Setting the Stage

1

Games? Really?

IN 1982, John Carroll noticed people playing what was probably the first computer adventure game, "Colossal Cave." He observed then what we see now, people hunched over a computer spending hours figuring out how to get further in the game. He compared that observation to people who were giving up on something considerably more valuable to them, learning to use a word processor.

At that time, I had a job creating educational computer games for the Apple II and other, similar, machines. It was my first job out of college, and I'd already been bitten by the computers-and-learning bug badly enough that I'd designed my own major in it (back then, they didn't have such degrees). And, as a professional obligation mind you, I was playing computer games, including the "Colossal Cave" adventure. I was captured by the possibility of embedding important decisions in adventure games and creating learning environments.

And that is really what this book is about, the results of a twenty-plus–year journey from that point, driven by a belief that learning can be fun. My understanding has been refined through research and trial-by-fire, and also buttressed with evidence. I heard the phrase "hard fun," and realized that is what I mean. It's fun, in the sense that you're engaged, there is a story that you care about, and you have the power to act; it's hard in that it's not trivial—there is sufficient challenge to keep you on your toes. And I most emphatically do *not* want you to infer that I mean the types of games where we put drill and kill, er, drill and practice, into game-based window dressing. I mean something more profound, more important, and more useful. But that is all to come.

To start, my plea is for you to stop doing e-learning the old way. That is, rewriting PowerPoint files and PDFs into online text (whether "gussied up" with graphics, photos, videos, or not) and multiple-choice knowledge tests (whether jazzed up with drag-and-drop or not). Or putting narrated slide presentations up on the Web. Yes, you can do that, and sometimes you have to (because of cost or time pressures). But stop first, and consider the alternatives. Understand that making things interesting can make them more effective, if you know how (and can interfere with learning if you don't), and that there are low roads that give you a lot of benefit for low investment as well as the high road. Then you can make an informed choice.

We are not, *cannot* be, about designing content. A fundamental perspective I want you to take away is that we are designing *experiences*. If nothing else, start thinking not about creating content but about designing learner environments and architecting experiences. It has become clear to me that this is a fundamental point. You have to start thinking about putting the learners into a context where they have to make decisions, understand why those decisions are important, want to make those decisions, and know that there are consequences of those decisions.

If you don't, you're likely to be dooming your audience to ineffective and, really, user-abusive learning. You don't have to make boring e-learning. Yet that is what I see, reliably and repeatedly. And it's not just me, the evidence is pretty consistent: when it comes to online learning, content people are staying away in droves. That has been the message from the analysts, the users, and the marketplace.

Of course, we'd like to develop richly engaging games that address key learning outcomes and are wildly fun, but even if we had the budget, would we know how? Or can we develop engaging learning on the average shoestring budget? I'll argue yes, absolutely, to both (and there are ways to boost that budget).

It is not because the content developers are not trying; it is because the elements of engagement are not understood. And it's not just a matter of putting entertainment and education folks in a room and locking the door. You have to understand the elements of both and find the alignment.

Let me put a stake in the ground here. *It is hard to do good education.* That is why people spend years learning how to do it. Even then, not all do more than follow the prescriptions and keep a finger on the pulse of the industry to improve their practice. *It is also hard to do good entertainment.* For every movie in Hollywood that is a hit, there are four or five that don't succeed. The same is true in the game industry (though I understand the ratios are even worse). *It is doubly hard to do both together.* Coordinating the elements requires a balancing act between the two, which can be well nigh impossible if you don't know how they work together (many assume that education and engagement are irreconcilable). *Yet it is more than doubly worthwhile.*

If you look at the elements that lead to learning, and put them in correspondence with the elements that lead to engagement, you'll see that they can be aligned and become mutually synergistic. By using that framework as guidance, you can systematically design learning that is both more effective and engaging. That is the thesis of this book.

Learning can, and should, be hard fun.

Engaging Experiences

At its best, learning is a wildly enjoyable experience. There are joyous discoveries, satisfied completions, and sudden recognitions. Think of children in that magic time of childhood before school undermines their intrinsic curiosity. All of us have interests about which we learn for no other reward than our own personal satisfaction. Whether it is a team sport such as baseball or an individual activity like fishing, a hobby such as collecting or crafts, or a personal pursuit such as philosophy or politics, in the pursuit of this informal learning we may be remarkably persistent in the face of adversity. We will learn by reading, by talking with people, perhaps by Web searching, buying books, watching specials, or joining societies.

However, this isn't what most people think of when they think of learning, particularly when it is codified as education or training. You're likely to get somewhat different responses: "I haven't time"; "Let me just read a book"; or "Not more school!" Drop-out rates for online learning have been listed as high as 80 percent. A renowned business school theorist suggests that what motivates people to take training is fear of being unable to perform, rather than any intrinsic value.

If you think that learning has to be "read this and take the test," then you haven't been paying attention to what's known about how we learn. The evidence is that learning is more effective if it attracts the attention and interest of the learner, is obviously relevant, requires action on the part of the learner, and is contextualized so that the learner understands how and when to apply it. In short, we need to address the emotional side of the learning as well as the knowledge side.

What we want is learning that engages the learner, but what we have is learning that bores or confuses the learner. Here, *engagement* is the word used to describe the situation when learners are captured, heart and mind, in learning—or to use formal terms, are cognitively and affectively connected to the learning experience. The best learning experiences generally available are either high-fidelity simulations or interactive sessions with skilled facilitators. However, most learning experiences involve heavy use of text, too many knowledge-test assessments, and facilitators who might care but are not so skilled as is needed.

Let me be clear, I'm not talking about game shows or gussied-up drill and practice. I am not advocating putting lipstick on the pig of fact-based learning. Instead, I am talking about the type of learning environment where you have a challenging goal set in a believable theme, and you must struggle to achieve the goal. We should be creating a learning environment where we transform our learning objectives to important behaviors, where contexts are meaningful to the learner, and where the decisions are consequential. These are the learning experiences that will make a difference, and they are what we should be shooting for.

Let me also acknowledge that I do not believe that these engaging learning experiences will (or should be expected to), by themselves, lead to learning. I advocate discussion around the experience, and connecting learner actions to the underlying concept. As yet, computers are not quite capable of supporting such dialogue. Self-directed learners may be capable of facilitating their own reflection, but it's not the way to bet (though I believe strongly that meta-learning, or learning to learn, is a key leverage point for the future). So although such environments are not sufficient, they are necessary; we need engaging experiences to motivate learners to attend to the content, give them rich practice opportunities, and provide fodder for discussion and refinement of their understanding.

Why Engagement?

Why should learning be hard fun? Surely, learners should buckle down and do what they need to do to acquire the necessary skills. Perhaps in an ideal world learners would be motivated and self-directed. We know, however, that having the pull of a challenging learning experience is still an advantage.

As long as engagement doesn't hurt, it's a positive. It doesn't have to help; as long as it doesn't interfere it can be argued to be valuable (of course, if the cost isn't too high). For instance, the Masie Center found that 70 percent of survey respondents would be *very* interested in a learning process that has computer games. I'll bet most folks developing learning would be thrilled to have 70 percent of their audience heading into the learning experience very interested.

People intuitively think that learning through games ought to be better, but is there any evidence? Although I won't be academic throughout (though there will be times), let me briefly review some findings. Work on cognitive science, education, anthropology, and practical experience guide the view that engagement enhances learning (when done right).

Some cognitive research either directly demonstrates or indirectly suggests the value of adding engagement to learning. Mark Lepper of Stanford University has investigated motivation in learning and in a key experiment showed that adding story enhancements to mathematics instruction improved outcomes (Lepper & Cordova, 1992). We can also use some inferences from the work of Phil Johnson-Laird of the Psychology Unit in Cambridge, who found that complex decisions are made more tractable by the addition of concrete context (e.g., Johnson-Laird, Legrenzi, & Legrenzi, 1972), which is part of the engagement process. Jean Lave at the University of California at Berkeley (1988) cites work on Brazilian street kids who can't seem to be taught mathematics, yet are actually quite good at doing calculation in the monetary tasks they perform to survive (showing motivational effects on learning).

We also see significant evidence in learning theory. The anchored instruction approach of John Bransford and his colleagues at Vanderbilt (Cognition and Technology Group, 1990) has had success in teaching a variety of core curricula such as mathematics through rich media and story. Jeroen Van Merriënboer's (1997) work on teaching complex skills suggests that we need full practice in simulated environments. Roger Schank's work on goal-based scenarios indicates the need for a goal and an exploratory environment to drive learning (Schank & Cleary, 1995). The entire focus of Howard Barrows's problem-based learning (Barrows, 1986), and case studies such as Harvard Business School's pedagogy, is to help make the learning more concrete and meaningful.

There's more pragmatic evidence as well. The military has a significant investment in rich simulations as training tools. Institutes continue to be founded to investigate games and training or learning. The Massachusetts Institute of Technology has one of the newest, and the University of Southern California has one as well. A surfeit of new books also talk about the need for games or simulations as learning environments: Marc Prensky, Clark Aldrich, James Gee, the list goes on. By the way, I'll differentiate between games and simulations (and approximations thereto) later on, but briefly, *simulations* rely on underlying models, not prescribed branches, and *games* are simulations with the aesthetic tuned to create an optimal level of engagement.

Finally, as Donald Norman's book *Emotional Design* points out, the effect of the experience adds to our ability to think and perform. As we begin to explore how emotional experience affects our cognition, the picture increasingly shows that the aesthetics matter. If this is indeed the case, we need to exploit this opportunity to our advantage. We can design learning experiences that have positive effect and have reasons to believe that is more effective for learning.

Games for learning are not just a guilty pleasure! The evidence is clear that rich environments and story lines are more engaging and more effective. But the real reason to investigate this comes from the second half of that claim. We need more effective learning. Why?

The Learning-Doing Continuum

Our goal is not to help people learn. That's a tactic. If we said people need to learn *X* and then made sure that happened, we wouldn't be doing our job. In organizations, the direction is no longer to hypothesize needs but to justify the cost. And the industry has moved beyond return-on-investment arguments. It's not about showing that improvement happens as an outcome of the training. Or even counting the dollar benefits of the outcomes. Instead, the goal now for training is to target and improve the key performance indicators of the organization. This trend is currently also reflected in the metrics associated with schools, though I hope that schools will soon move to a more realistic way of assessment that targets what learners actually can do (for example, portfolios of work) and not just what they know.

No, the goal is clear: we must help people *do*. And that, at the end of the day, is the strongest argument for focusing on engagement in learning, because learning designed to incorporate engagement is more effective.

So why is our learning so dry? A widely cited Forrester report (Hogg, 2002) found that 75 percent of e-learners do not finish their courses. This is *not* because the courses are engaging learning experiences. We're following the prescriptions of instructional design, which we know is empirically based to ensure learning outcomes. What is new are the results of cognitive research (mentioned above) that suggest extensions to our learning design. This research begins to give us ideas of what we need in an environment. What hasn't been presented to date is a reliable way to get there.

A learning environment has to be designed properly to incorporate engagement that integrates with effectiveness. The problem is figuring out how to do it, particularly under real-world constraints, and seeing whether there are intermediate steps that can give us leverage when we simply can't justify the development of a full game engine. Just putting educational people and entertainment people in the same room isn't going to do it, because they don't have a shared vocabulary or any understanding of how their work aligns and synergizes. That there have been more failures than successes is not a surprise. Yet if we do understand both sides, we can make them work together to accomplish this goal of better learning experience *and* better learning.

Is this approach appropriate for all learning objectives? Yes and no. If your learning objectives are about knowledge—for example, does someone know *x* or *y*—you don't need to create engaging scenarios (though you can ramp up the engagement with quiz show–type trappings). However, I believe we mistakenly think that knowledge alone will solve our problem, when usually we need that knowledge to be actionable—and then we do need an engaged approach. Sometimes you will want to have lower-level knowledge automated, so that you're equipped to take on more complex decisions, but I believe in putting the decisions first to motivate learners to recognize why they need the more-rote practice. Then you can make that more enjoyable, too, but the focus has to be on the ability to *do*. And that requires focus on creating a learning experience.

There is a hierarchy of knowledge, as Tony O'Driscoll (2003) has pointed out. As you enter a new domain, at the base or bottom position of expertise the knowledge is fairly well agreed upon. As you move up to greater expertise, you get to areas where understanding is still being negotiated and the learning is more through communication and collaboration. The approach here works better when there is agreement about the right approach, although you could allow such an environment to have an ambiguous ending as long as you can create a vehicle for dialogue afterward. However, as I reiterate later, engaged learning is not designed to be a total learning solution but an important component of practice. Reflection is still best left to mechanisms outside the game environment (ideally, with mentors and peers). However, I argue that the environments I'm talking about, the experiences I'm suggesting we can and should design, are the right sort of practice environments for most behaviors and learning goals when we know what we want to achieve.

The Payoff

Why should we do this? Although we don't yet have the data to support quantitative justification, we can cite several qualitative reasons. First and foremost is that our learning will be more effective. This approach, done properly, leads to greater retention over time and transfer to appropriate situations. Second, it increases the likelihood of learners' continuing to the end and achieving the desired outcomes. If they like it, they will play. Third, it will increase learner morale. Who wouldn't be happier with a learning experience that sticks and creates an engaging experience?

Let's walk through a situation. You've got an organizational change that is critical to the success of the company, say a shift to a customer focus (why is that a *new* concept?). You approach it the traditional way: the CEO addresses the troops about the importance. PowerPoint slides are created to deliver the details to departments companywide. These slides are rewritten into Web-based content, with some multiple-choice questions tacked on. The employees are sent an e-mail pointing them to the URL for the course and told that it's important. They dutifully start, are bored stiff, are distracted by an important job issue, and never go back. If their manager even bothers to check, they successfully argue that it was a case of finishing the course or closing the Acme deal (substitute other appropriate departmental crisis). The change doesn't take hold, the company continues doing business as usual, and eventually another imperative business change is announced.

Now consider an alternative. The content is re-imagined as a game, where the player starts in a customer-facing role. It's not heavily produced, it's done with some dialogue and some stock photos, but it's heavily designed, with lots of thought about how people will go wrong, what the consequences should be, and how to ensure that the difficulty starts low but gradually increases. The players get to make choices about how to behave, but the choices aren't obvious. They fail but get just enough of a hint to think they know what they need to do next. And they fail again. Yet the story is believable enough, interesting enough, and the outcomes linked closely enough to the business that they "get" why it's important to succeed at this. They struggle through, going to portals to download relevant documents, until they succeed. They now know the need. They talk about the game with their colleagues, and employee interest in it spreads word-of-mouth. And more important, the learning sticks and the organization slowly takes on the desired characteristics and moves ahead in a strategic direction.

This isn't fantasy; it can happen. It's a different way of learning, and one we need. And just in case it sounds overwhelming, there are baby steps along the way. You can tap into the power of learning like this fairly simply, but if it's really important or you have a large audience, you can use the effectiveness of the approach to justify the more major investment. Again, however, you don't get this by just putting game designers and instructional designers into a room together. You need to understand how to align and exploit the two sides, but there is alignment, and it can be leveraged.

Road Map

And that, in a nutshell, is the premise of this book: that there is a synergistic alignment of engagement and learning effectiveness that we can exploit and systematically implement to improve our learning solutions. The trick is to design our learning in a new way, a way that puts learners into the position of making decisions that make the content meaningful and are aligned with how they need to apply the knowledge. My claim is that there is not a learning objective for which we cannot design a game (but I reserve the right to raise the objective to a meaningful level).

The concomitant focus of this book is how to redesign learning into compelling and effective learning experiences. Note that the book is not about how to produce these designs. There are many ways to do it, and the inherent trade-offs between choosing to use a fixed branching solution or a flexible rule-based engine are related to the context of implementation and not upon the design. I believe the hard task is coming up with the design; once that's done, there are a variety of ways to get it built. In fact, as a reviewer suggested, you absolutely have to have the design nailed down before you think about how to produce it, as the design will influence your choice of implementation tools. (It's too easy to let the tool dictate the design, and that way lies educational ineffectiveness.) Further, considerable savings in production can be sustained from spending the energy in design up front. Challenging questions can engage learners such that high production values are not required to maintain interest (although, of course, they can add to the experience if aligned to the learning, and ideally are also included).

To get there, I briefly review learning (for those coming from the engagement side) and engagement (for those coming from the learning side). In both cases, I want a shared foundation. From there, I demonstrate the alignment and use it to take a first pass at enhancing traditional instructional design. I then proceed from that, through a series of incremental improvements, to the structure of full games. I place this developed framework in the context of a usable design process, derived from familiar design processes and with indications of how existing processes can be amended rather than replaced. In the process, I cover some practical hints and tips (really, lessons learned). I also point to some of the future directions I see coming, before wrapping up.

Engaged learning is doable. I saw the connection between computers and learning in college when I got a job maintaining the computer records of the office managing the math and science tutoring I'd been doing. As mentioned earlier, I saw the link between computer games and learning when my first job out of college was designing and programming educational computer games. I spent a large part of my graduate student career looking at every form of what makes experiences effective for learning. I looked at instructional design, developmental psychology, cognitive learning, and behavioral learning. I even looked at *machine* learning! As part of my research then and subsequently, I also examined the elements that contribute to an engaging experience, across drama, fiction, experiential psychology, interface design, and, of course, computer games. I discovered an alignment that is teachable, systematic, and effective. And I've had a chance to hone my theorizing through practice.

The road ahead is straight, but it has some steep spots. To truly understand and apply this approach, you have to understand learning and engagement reasonably deeply. Therefore, Chapters Two and Three, and their integration, Chapter Four, are somewhat theoretical. And from time to time in other places I similarly take some time to develop a framework (for example, Chapter Six). As a consequence, although this book primarily addresses e-learning, the principles are applicable more broadly to the category of experience design, interaction design, and other recent buzzwords. Similarly, I hope the audience can include instructional designers, programmers, game designers, trainers, interaction designers, and so forth.

Chapter Two reviews traditional instructional design, enhances it with cognitive results, and derives a model that reflects where many learning models are converging. Some elements are extracted that highlight effective learning. In principle those who understand learning can skip this chapter, but I request that you at least review the convergent model so we start with some common terminology.

Chapter Three does a similar review of elements of engagement, ultimately extracting elements that characterize an engaging experience. This chapter could be skipped by those with experience in game design, though again I request at least reviewing the synthesis, at least to share vocabulary.

Chapter Four is the key to the approach, where the elements of engagement and learning are aligned. It points to some principles to guide effective outcomes. This is where we discover, and elaborate, the key synergy.

Chapter Five is a practical chapter of models that can be used. The chapter reviews several levels for applying the principles to learning goals. This discussion starts with very small modifications to existing approaches, and culminates in a full engine-driven game.

Chapter Six is a how-to chapter that walks you through the background of design. It then derives a systematic process that starts with gathering objectives, and works through the details of nailing down a design that is both engaging and effective. You could start here, even with the section that is the synergy of the game and learning design processes, if you really need to get something done, but I hope you will be intrigued enough to go back and "get" the underpinning framework. I don't think you will be equipped to wrestle with the nuances that will arise if you don't understand the principles.

Chapter Seven is another practical chapter that goes over a laundry list of pragmatic issues to consider and lessons learned. I toss in a number of thoughts and ideas here that address the reality of doing what I'm talking about, which don't necessarily arise from the theory.

Chapter Eight is a forward-looking chapter that talks about some trends that are emerging and some possible new directions. Here's where we see what the future of engaged learning might be.

Chapter Nine sums up where we've been and gives us direction in moving forward.

A case study is used to help convey the principles in Chapter Four, and one each is used to demonstrate the different levels of application. These case studies are illustrated in some cases with screenshots, but idiosyncratically. This has to do with the difficulty in obtaining permission to use the relevant images. People were happy in principle to provide them, but when it came time for official signatures, in several cases legalities and permissions resulted in protracted negotiations. As there is a timetable to produce a book, some of the permissions had to be abandoned. However, I've tried to include some representations that convey, if not the final product, some of the development process.

YOU'LL ALSO FIND SOME SIDE COMMENTS LOOKING LIKE THIS

I care passionately about helping people improve their ability to solve the problems they face, and learning new skills is the key. There is more good content that needs to be developed than I can handle, so I want more people to have the skills to do this. Even small improvements will help create the groundswell of interest and examples we need to fundamentally change not only the vast majority of what is seen out there, but the way we think about learning design.

Hence, this book. Please, read, use, design better learning, and make us all happier and better off! *Learning can, and should, be hard fun.*

2

Learning Basics

WHAT DO WE KNOW ABOUT LEARNING? Quite a bit, actually, though there is a lot we're still researching. For instance, we know that certain elements increase the likelihood of achieving our learning outcomes. However, we have to look to the evidence, not just our intuitions; just because you've gone to school doesn't mean you're an expert on teaching (sad to say, this view seems all too prevalent). In this chapter, I cover traditional approaches to learning, introduce some aspects that have proven useful, and use that to drive a richer model. I then extract some elements that have been shown to enhance learning outcomes. If you're experienced in learning and instruction theory, you may be able to skip right to the synthesis section about a convergent model. Although contributions are sketched here, I recommend reading the original to get all the nuances.

Note that my choice of references is somewhat personal. These references are touchstones I use to help indicate the breadth of materials covered here. They are not to be considered by any means comprehensive, but rather provide some grounding for the concepts brought together. I'm very much the practitioner, not the theorist, applying what I can use.

Regardless, this discussion is still inherently a bit theoretical. I've tried to distill it down to a minimum, but there's only so much one can do. As a consequence, I briefly point to a wide variety of ideas. They all have merit, and I recommend going back to the originals (even if you discover I occasionally played a little "fast and loose" with them to suit my own ends). If you don't want to read the derivation, that's okay. But if you don't come from a learning theory background, I'd recommend it; you can't do successful e-learning game design without some understanding of the elements of learning. However, do please at least review the convergent model and the final elements. I will be referring to and building upon this framework.

Instructional Design

What is known about facilitating learning and associated design processes to systematically transform learning goals into learning experiences has been developed under the rubric of instructional design. At its core, individual learning is about engaging in activity, encountering a problem and reflecting to create an abstract conception, and then testing that conception through more activity in an ongoing cycle (see Figure 2-1).

Figure 2-1. Learning Cycle.

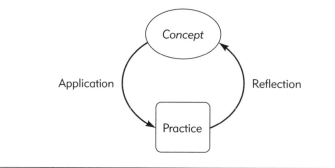

Refining that model from general learning to successful instruction, we start with abstract conceptions we create for learners. In addition, we provide examples to guide the application. Then we must include practice and reflection on that practice to link their practice back to the conception (see Figure 2-2).

Figure 2-2. Instruction Cycle.

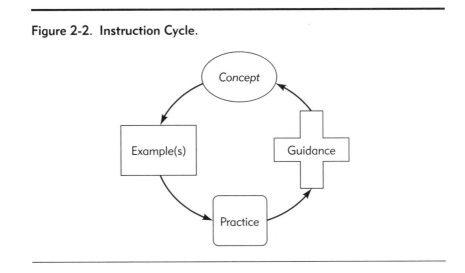

For any learning critical enough to justify the investment in time, we also tune that conception through practice into automated procedures. Such automation of a skill provides one the benefit of being able to perform the skill without conscious thought (for instance, reading). Instructional design goes beyond this to stipulate some criteria around the different elements of concept, example, practice, and so forth.

Instructional design (also known as instructional system design or ISD) is basically a series of steps to identify needs, state those needs in a usefully precise way, and align elements of content to address those needs, as well as assess the outcome. The origins in behavioral psychology have provided an empirical basis and rigor that have led to confidence in the outcomes.

Perpetrators

A number of people have been influential in framing what is known about instructional design. These fall into the traditional foundation frameworks and additions or extensions to the work.

Initial Frameworks. Major theorists in the field of instructional design include Benjamin Bloom (Bloom & Krathwohl, 1956) and Robert Gagné (Gagné, Briggs, & Wager, 1992). Their work lays out how one systematically proceeds to characterize and develop learning. Others have elaborated particular elements. David Merrill (1983) in particular has built upon and elaborated their work.

Bloom. Benjamin Bloom developed a taxonomy of types of knowledge we can have and use (Bloom & Krathwohl, 1956). The notion of identifying different levels of application is an important step in thinking about how to teach and what type of performance we want to achieve.

These types of knowledge help us determine what we want our learners to be able to do with the knowledge. For our purposes, we want to quickly dismiss lower levels and work on the higher levels of the taxonomy, and for good reasons. Others have subsequently provided other taxonomies, but the concept of a skill or knowledge taxonomy is a useful distinction.

Gagné. Robert Gagné has a similar taxonomy, but the real contribution of his work was in specifying the elements necessary to achieve successful learning outcomes (Gagné, Briggs, & Wager, 1992). Gagné, with colleagues, posited elements of instruction as necessary for learning, including the aforementioned concepts, examples, practice, and so forth. These elements have formed the basis for learning content design.

I use my own characterization of the component elements in this book, but the concept of having discrete components is the basis for designing experiences necessary to achieve learning.

Extensions. Other theorists have elaborated these basics. Robert Mager (1975) has provided lasting guidance on how we should specify our learning goals. Charles Reigeluth (Reigeluth & Stein, 1983) has helped us understand how we should develop complex ideas. And John Keller (1983) raised the importance of considering the affective nature of learning.

Mager. Robert Mager (1975) rightly suggested that the learning gap to be addressed should be framed in terms of the performance outcomes desired from the learner. He indicated that the outcome of an intervention needs to be couched in the form of a learning objective that can be measured to see whether the outcome has been achieved. Two necessary elements are understanding the context(s) in which the performance is appropriate and metrics to objectively determine whether the performance has been successfully completed.

Reigeluth. Charles Reigeluth's elaboration theory suggests that the correct way to present learning is to start with the big picture to help orient the learner into the context before digging down into the details (Reigeluth & Stein, 1983). Although Reigeluth has a detailed model, the take-home message is to start with a simple version and gradually elaborate both in complexity and comprehensiveness until the knowledge or skill is fully elaborated and exercised. We will use this notion in addressing the complexity level of games.

Keller. John Keller (1983) has added an essential element to the instructional design model. Recognizing that the learner's mental state has an impact on learning, Keller's ARCS (Attention, Relevance, Confidence, & Satisfaction) model proposes that effective learning has to address the affective elements as well as the knowledge components. Keller wants to make sure learners are paying attention, understand why this information is important to them, are able to develop confidence in their ability, and are satisfied by the outcomes of the learning experience. These elements are a core component of achieving a successful learning experience.

Structure

As a consequence of the above influences, I propose a convergent list of elements for learning. These elements will be used as the basis for developing a learning experience. At a top level, the elements are

- (Objective)
- Introduction
- Concept
- Example(s)

- Practice

- Summary

I will elaborate this list both here and further on, but I first address the initial elements.

(Objective). While technically not a content element, no learning content can be developed until a learning objective is established. The important point is to have a detailed objective. It's very hard to define a meaningful learning experience unless you know what your intended outcome is, and for whom.

Introduction. Once you have identified your objective, you need to introduce the subject to the learner. As Gagné suggests, learners should be aware that this is a learning opportunity and that it is relevant to them; they should know what they should expect as outcomes and be able to activate relevant knowledge. These prerequisites are typically accomplished through presentation of the rationale for the learning, explicit linking to existing knowledge, and a statement of the objectives of the learning.

Concept. The actual content includes an underlying framework or model, through a concept presentation. This is typically a lexical presentation, whether verbal or text, sometimes accompanied by a graphic of the model or a set of steps.

Example(s). To help bridge the gap from abstract conceptualization to concrete application, examples of the concept applied to various contexts help illustrate how to use the associated knowledge or skills. These examples allow the learner to relate the principles to practice.

Practice. To allow learners to internalize the knowledge, as well as assess their learning, learners should have to perform the behavior in the context and compare their performances to the level specified in the objective. Feedback is necessary here to allow learners or mentors to understand the learners' performances and address any deficiencies. Performance also allows you to determine when instruction can stop, as the learner has achieved the learning objectives.

Summary. At the end of the learning, we typically summarize what the learner has learned and point to further directions if the learner wishes to know more.

Cognitive Enhancements

Cognitive research has helped us extend the initial characterization of designing for learning. We revisit the goals of learning again before visiting several significant theorists.

Goals

The goal of learning, finally, is to achieve a change in behavior that is retained over time and applies in all relevant situations, even if not seen in the learning situation. The cognitive revolution, a cross-disciplinary rebellion against a strict behaviorist stance, had its origins in the mid 1950s and eventually started having an impact on learning in the 1960s and 1970s. This was a change in philosophical orientation toward examining the necessary internal elements that would lead to exhibited behavior. This movement has subsequently flowered into several related approaches that have had positive influences on our learning, such as situated cognition, connectionist approaches, and more.

We use the term *retention* to talk about learning that persists beyond the learning situation and can be applied at appropriate opportunities on an ongoing basis. We use the term *transfer* to characterize learning applied to appropriate situations not covered in the learning situation. Our goals of learning, then, are to foster retention and transfer of knowledge and skills.

Retention is fostered by comprehension and practice. We need to understand the appropriate framework, and we need sufficient practice to automate the skill to the level necessary to successfully address each application opportunity with the desired degree of expertise. We know that spaced practice leads to better retention, so spreading a number of practice opportunities over several days is more effective than accomplishing the same number on one day. We also know that the more meaningful and motivating the practice is, the higher the retention.

Transfer is developed through practice across contexts. To the extent possible, this practice should come from as widely disparate contexts as possible. The cognitive rationale for this is that by having the abstract concept framework as the only invariant across the practice opportunities, the learner has a better chance to infer the underlying framework.

Thus, our goal is to provide sufficient, meaningful practice to help ensure that the learning will be retained and recognized as appropriate to apply to all relevant situations.

Perpetrators

Some major approaches in learning models include cognitive apprenticeship, four-component instructional design, and goal-based scenarios. Elements from other approaches also play a role.

Cognitive Apprenticeship. A framework that arose from abstraction across several approaches is the cognitive apprenticeship model of Allan Collins, John Seely Brown, and Susan Newman (1989). After reviewing the work of Anne Brown and Anne-Marie Palincsar in reading, Alan Shoenfeld on mathematics, and Marlene Scardemalia and Carl Bereiter in writing, Collins, Brown, and Newman posited a process of modeling the desired behavior, providing opportunities to practice (with support through simplified problems, called scaffolding, which is gradually removed), and reflecting on performance to help refine and cement the learning.

The cognitive apprenticeship framework provides some specific elaboration of the elements identified from instructional design. The examples need not only demonstrate the application but also make explicit the thought processes that are being used to make decisions (a process I call "cognitive annotation"). One of the common omissions by instructors is failing to illustrate the alternatives before choosing a step. It also is desirable to demonstrate making mistakes and recovering from them. *Learners sometimes believe that if they do not get it right the first time, they're failures, but in reality experts backtrack and repair regularly.* Showing recovery from mistakes helps learners build self-esteem and cope when things go wrong, as often happens. Further, practice activities may need to be simplified initially and then gradually increased. And there need to be reflection opportunities for learners to compare their performance with the abstract conceptualization. Reflection should encompass more than just feedback; ideally it should review across all the practice opportunities as a more overarching consideration of performance.

I discovered cognitive apprenticeship early in my graduate career, and it has been a guiding framework for my work. As I read new stuff that resonated with my thoughts, my students would remind me that it was already in cognitive apprenticeship! I believe that as many approaches adapt to accommodate new outcomes, they're converging on a model. And that model is essentially where cognitive apprenticeship has been all along.

4C/ID. A recent framework is Jeroen Van Merriënboer's four-component instructional design (4C/ID). In this work, Van Merriënboer (1997) has been concerned with the complex skills people need to acquire, and the fact that most combine well-understood knowledge-level objectives with ill-defined sequencing skills. He created a learning model that embeds knowledge-skill practice for those skills that need to be automated, and then embeds their use within a richer decision-making process. He has created what I think is a very good way to address the types of skills we need to focus on.

Goal-Based Scenarios. Roger Schank has been a proponent of a model called goal-based scenarios where learners face decisions in complex situations that they recognize are important (Schank & Cleary, 1995). These situations are designed to be difficult, and the learner is likely to initially fail before eventually succeeding. Schank wants to develop low-level knowledge skills by driving the learner to information resources available within or external to the learning environment, not by explicit instruction. This happens because learners are motivated to solve the problems as the environments focus on interesting and important skills for the learner, made contextually meaningful by setting them within a compelling scenario.

Extensions. A few other elements that extend the cognitive approach arise from particular approaches. Rand Spiro's cognitive flexibility theory (Spiro, Feltovich, Jacobson, & Coulson, 1992) suggests that, particularly for difficult or ill-defined concepts, multiple representations give learners greater success at finding a solution. John Carroll (1990), inspired by his insights from computer gaming, created minimalist instruction, an approach for developing training materials that suggests giving the learner some credit as an intelligent individual. Thus, the approach provides only the minimal instruction needed to "get" the concept, expecting the clear goals of the context to help provide structure to support the learner to succeed. John Bransford and team (Cognition and Technology Group, 1990) developed anchored instruction, in which stories set dilemmas, and suggest that the learning materials have to be meaningful to the learner.

Marcia Conner (2004) has recently introduced the notion of whole-body learning. She cites research about how neuropeptides pass information around the body without involving conscious awareness. Our emotional reactions to learning can interfere with the ability to effectively take advantage of information. Trainers and teachers are able to note our engagement in the classroom but programs cannot (as yet). We need to engage more of the body in learning, not just the mind. Otherwise, those little voices we hear ("Oh, I hate this stuff" or "I'm so bad at this") can undermine what we're trying to achieve. So we want to start with attracting the emotional commitment to the learning and then develop a more encompassing experience that invokes more of the physiological affect that will mimic (or exaggerate) the performance situation.

John Seely Brown and Allan Collins, both of cognitive apprenticeship fame, along with Paul Duguid, developed situated learning, which talks about how the learning skills have to be meaningful applications of the knowledge in a real context of practice (Brown, Collins, & Duguid, 1989). John Anderson's work on learning (as well as work on analogy) has pointed out the mechanisms necessary to achieve transfer, including how to use examples (Singley & Anderson, 1989). To support far transfer, examples and practice need to cover disparate scenarios to help abstract the underlying principle.

David Jonassen has been at the forefront of so-called constructivist approaches, which suggest that learners cannot be instructed but must develop their own understanding (Jonassen, Howland, Moore, & Marra, 2003). Consequently, learners need to be active in engaging with problems and developing hypotheses, and they must have feedback that helps them refine their models. This work has changed our notion of learning to emphasize the social nature of learning through dialogue between learners, and between learners and mentors, as the active process of learners refining their understanding.

Finally, Lev Vygotsky (1978), a Russian psychologist, developed a rich learning model based upon the social nature of learning. His model describes a zone of proximal development (commonly referred to as ZOPD), where learning occurs. Making a graph and starting with the area where the learner is fully competent, draw a line to where there are tasks that they can't accomplish even with help. In between is a range of tasks that the learner can accomplish with some help (again, scaffolding). It is in this area or zone that learning occurs.

A Convergent Model

Associated with instructional design are various philosophies that provide the basis for the different models. These philosophical differences are interesting and important, but there is an emergent model that integrates the best of the research. We now have an elaborated set of elements. Some of the elements above overlap, but the overlap merely serves to reinforce the convergent nature of the emergent model.

I'm going to suggest, as an abstraction across a number of the approaches, that the objective to be addressed by the learning needs to be of sufficient complexity to be interesting to the learner. This suggests that we need to move from *knowledge test,* where we ask learners whether they know the elements or can identify them, to a *knowledge application* level, where learners have to use the knowledge to solve a contextualized problem to make a discrimination—essentially to make a decision in the colloquial sense of the word. Formally, all forms of test items, such as true-false or multiple choice, are decisions, but colloquially, decisions are typically construed as situations in which an individual is in a context and has to make a decision that affects the world in some way. In other words, it's not about learning the difference between an *x* and a *y,* it's (at least) about distinguishing between *x*'s and *y*'s to accomplish a goal. I'll use the term *decisions* throughout the book to refer to the latter concept of meaningful goal-oriented choices.

Another inference is that we may need a more compelling introduction that dramatically illustrates why this knowledge is important. It can accomplish the goals that introductions need to accomplish (activating relevant knowledge, introducing objectives, explaining the role of the information) in a more compelling and meaningful way that addresses the learner emotionally as well as mentally.

Elements

This framework results in the following proposed elements:

- (Objective)

- Dramatic introduction
- Multiply represented concept
- Annotated examples
- Scaffolded practice
- Reflection

(Objective). The objective should be at least at a knowledge application level. It still needs metrics and audience specifications, but it should be at a meaningful level.

Dramatic Introduction. The introduction should include a compelling portrayal of the value of the knowledge, dramatic or humorous, ideally in a way that incorporates the relevant prior knowledge and indicates the outcomes. We need to address not only the learners' minds, but also their hearts; we need them to "get" why this is important, why they care, and let that motivation pull them through the course ahead.

Multiply Represented Concept. Conceptual material should be multiply represented by using text as well as diagrams, animations, and other illustrative ways of communication. We need to use multiple media, think of different ways of providing metaphors, and use different ways of communicating these metaphors to different types of learners.

Annotated Examples. Examples need to be annotated with the underlying thought processes that drive the decisions in sequencing steps in problem-solving, and be drawn from an appropriately diverse set of contexts. They should be contextualized so that they can be processed in the form of stories.

Scaffolded Practice. The practice opportunities need to be graduated in a way to develop expertise in appropriate chunks and also be spread across an appropriately diverse set of contexts.

Reflection. There should be time and support for reflecting on the practice opportunities that link their application back to the theoretical framework.

These elements are indicated in Figure 2-3.

Figure 2-3. Enhanced Instructional Design Model.

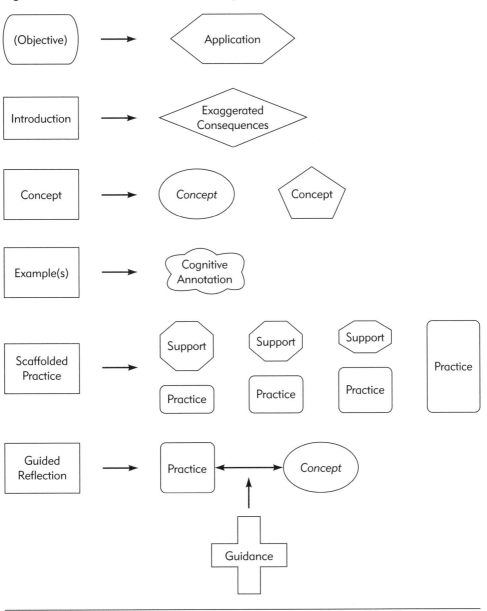

For each element, a graphic representation is included that is intended to emphasize the key point I'm highlighting above (on the learning style chart, I'm definitely abstract and visual). The objective should focus on knowledge application. The introduction should highlight (perhaps with exaggeration) the consequences of *not* having this knowledge (or, conversely, the benefits of *having* the knowledge). The concept should have multiple representations. The examples should be cognitively annotated. The practice should start simply with lots of support; gradually the support should be removed and the full practice handed off to the learner. And reflection should provide guided support for linking the learner's performance back to the underlying concept.

Elements Redux

We can also take a different cut through the elements proposed by highlighting some of the elements that contribute to successful learning. This list selects out, across the approaches, the core elements that create experiences that contribute to learning:

- Contextualized
- Clear goal
- Appropriate challenge
- Anchored
- Relevant
- Exploratory
- Active manipulation
- Appropriate feedback
- Attention-getting

The rationale for this cut will become clear.

Contextualized. Learning needs to be contextualized—put in concrete instances (and across relevant sample contexts to represent the appropriate breadth).

Clear Goal. Learners should know or discover what the outcome is they need to achieve.

Appropriate Challenge. A learning experience has to be pitched at the correct level for learning to occur. Learning happens in the zone where we're "stretched" just the right amount.

Anchored. The learning examples need to be real practice instances in which the knowledge being used is meaningful to the story.

Relevant. The learning also needs to be meaningful to the learners.

Exploratory. Learners have to explore the material, not simply have it presented to them.

Active Manipulation. The learners have to make decisions and take action.

Appropriate Feedback. Learners need feedback on the actions they take.

Attention-Getting. The material has to have a level of interest to the learners.

Summary

The elements listed in the convergent model give us a handle on what forms of content we need to develop, whereas the second version highlights how learners need to act and the experiences they need, to deliver learning outcomes that achieve our initial goals: (1) retention and (2) transfer to appropriate situations. It's the latter perspective that shapes what we're going to do, but I did want to ensure that when we elaborate the experience with resources (content), we'll be building from a point of strength.

To put it another way, we need learning experiences that provide interesting goals set in meaningful contexts in which learners explore and act to solve problems that are pitched at the right level. Their actions should result in meaningful feedback from the world about the consequences of those actions. Further, the learning experiences should gradually increase in difficulty until learners have achieved the final level of performance and accomplished the goal. Within these learning experiences, learners will need multiply represented concepts, annotated examples, and guided reflection, but the point is to focus on the experience. And to do that, we need to understand what creates a compelling experience.

3

Experience Basics

CAN WE DEFINE THE ELEMENTS that make an experience engaging? The received answer is no. For example, both the film industry and the computer game industry use a business model in which a few hits cover the costs of many flops. Given the millions of dollars at stake, it is reasonable to expect that a systematic approach to successful development would be used if available. So it is hard to suggest that there is any recipe or procedure that guarantees engagement.

That is not to say, however, that we should not try. We can do a lot better than random chance. Following some principles can give us a good start, and then it is recognized that tuning and "tweaking" the outcome can improve the outcome. Although movies are hard to tweak, games are more amenable to adjustment. In the game industry, competitive timelines and large budgets can prematurely constrain development, whereas with smaller budgets, even though time remains important, trade-offs in necessary quality versus time can be considered more flexibly.

And to be honest, learning that is not dreary and dull is a much lower threshold than achieving commercial success (though this is no admission that we cannot achieve that goal). Entertainment productions are in the commercial arena, where the outcomes of marketing are not entirely predictable, whereas in many cases we have a captive audience, and our goals are more modest.

Just as the last chapter reviewed learning theory, this chapter reviews different approaches to creating engaging experiences. With a more disparate set of sources, the approach is more mixed but still provides a list of elements that characterize engagement. It's also a bit theoretical again, I'm afraid. However, you really do have to understand both learning and engagement to successfully create effective and engaging learning experiences. If you're an expert on the topic, you can skip all but the synthesis, but I'd like to suggest that the eclectic matter drawn upon might be of interest.

Engagement

In exploring elements of engagement, I have considered sources from several areas: first, psychological investigations into what makes compelling experiences; second, computer interface design, specifically regarding elements of engagement in computer-mediated experiences; and third, the ultimate area of computer-generated engagement, computer game design itself. That's not all, but it's representative of the elements on which I have drawn. Let's start, however, by looking at categories of games.

Genres

Although there are so-called genre-busting titles that cross boundaries, we can identify some major categories of games. The benefits are twofold: to understand some of the dimensions of difference, and to have some templates to pull off the shelf to match our needs.

We should also distinguish between game platforms. Initially there were the arcade games, featuring dedicated hardware. Then came the home computers and the games upon them. Some of those computers were more game machines with dedicated graphics hardware; the Atari machines and the Amiga are two examples. The market split, and on one hand are the so-called *consoles*, the gam-

The console games have fewer input options and require learning complex combinations of controls as part of the skill. Consequently, they're not necessarily ideal for learning games. However, if the interface is kept simple, and the focus is on the challenge of using the simple interface, there are some very interesting opportunities (or if the time spent in learning a more complex interface has a significant learning outcome that justifies the extra time). For instance, the early graphic adventure games had only a limited set of navigation and object manipulation actions: you could move (north, south, east, and west) and take, drop, or use things. Interfaces for such games evolved with more complex options, but at the core little more was necessary, yet many complex story lines were built around this type of interface (a suite from ICOM, including "Déjà Vu," "Shadow-Gate," and "Uninvited" were early favorites of mine).

My dissertation research was on analogical reasoning (using a model from one area to solve a problem in another, an approach that is suggested to form the foundation of much of our problem-solving and learning), and as a side task during my postdoctoral fellowship, I developed a game that required analogical reasoning to solve by using just such an interface. You played a cultural anthropologist, and in the game you read your journal notes, and then the story line put you in a position where you faced obstacles that were structurally similar but the details were different. If you could do the analogical inference, you could solve the puzzle.

Although the straightforward approach is to embed your learning goals into game experiences, I am still interested in putting more general problem-solving skills, like analogy, into such environments too. My children are currently playing and enjoying some of the commercial entertainment titles such as "Pajama Sam." They do require problem-solving skills but are lacking the reflection mentioned in the previous chapter (so many of these games claim to build problem-solving skills, but requiring such skills and actually developing them are two different things). Although supporting development problem-solving skills is naturally a role for parents, it is not necessarily an ability parents have and there's often no support for them. Further, I think that there are ways in which such games could develop such skills. Anyone interested in pursuing it?

ing platforms such as GameCube and PlayStation with their dedicated gaming architectures and controllers, as well as their handheld equivalents; on the other hand are the games that run on the more generic personal computers.

Personal computers now include multiplayer versions of games that start on your computer but then connect through the Internet to other players (this is touted as a new capability for consoles as well). And there are games that are played exclusively online. Within those constraints, we can have different genres of games, with different educational potential.

Action. Essentially the original category, action games include running around or manipulating things under time constraints. These games require coordination and reflexes.

Fighting. A version of an action game, fighting games feature characters in martial arts combat.

Driving or Flying. Another action game, these games simulate driving or flying vehicles, often in competition. The Microsoft Flight Simulator was supposed to be just that, a simulator, but it came to be played as a game because the challenge and fantasy were appealing.

Sports. Sports games mimic popular individual or team sports, such as football or skiing. These games could help players develop the mental skills involved in such sports.

3D Shooter. These are games where the view is first person and you move through a simulated environment using weapons to shoot at enemies. The first-person viewpoint requires some navigational capabilities.

Card or Board. These are electronic versions of familiar games such as solitaire and chess. Some of these have strategic components.

Strategy. This category includes a variety of games in which the story line requires prioritizing and allocating resources to gradually grow and conquer. Games are often set in historic lands or in space. They may require negotiation and navigation skills, as well as planning.

Fantasy Role Playing. Fantasy Role-Playing Games (RPGs) are games in which players control a character or team of characters that combat and gain skills over time. They can have embedded puzzles.

Adventure. These are games in which the character typically explores and must figure out how to overcome puzzles to advance.

Multiplayer. Some of the games, including 3D shooters, fantasy role playing, and strategy, have developed capabilities to allow players to play against one another.

Massively Multiplayer Online Role-Playing Games. Massively multiplayer online role-playing games (MMORPG) have persistent worlds where many players come and go as they please, interact, and pursue goals individually or in groups. The social aspects have as yet unexplored potential for learning.

Combinations. Combinations of various types of games are well known; for instance, games that combine elements of RPGs with adventure or that mix driving with a 3D shooter.

Sources

Having considered different genres of games, now we will look at the different sources on elements of engagement. These include investigations of experience, narrative, human-computer interaction, and game design.

Experience

In the psychological consideration of experience, Mihaly Csikszentmihalyi has been the seminal figure. He has investigated *peak* experiences, ones that give the feeling of being "in the zone" (Csikszentmihalyi & Csikszentmihalyi, 1988). He has termed this the experience of *flow*. A flow state ensues when one is engaged in self-controlled, goal-related, meaningful actions. A key element of flow is the management of challenge, having it above the normal requirements of individuals but within their capability. There must be a goal that can be achieved, dependent on learner actions, and with immediate feedback.

Tom Malone, in his Ph.D. thesis (with Mark Lepper), investigated the elements that make computer games fun to play (Malone, 1981). He posited four elements that were abstracted from his research: challenge, fantasy, curiosity, and control. *Challenge* required a reasonable level of difficulty, *fantasy* meant having a compelling setting for the game action, *curiosity* included the games' having random events and not being completely deterministic, and *control* meant that the learners had choices to make.

Narrative

We also find elements of engagement in narrative, as exemplified in story and theater (including film). Joseph Campbell (1972, 1991) has looked at the myths and stories found in cultures around the world and has abstracted commonalities. Others have analyzed the mechanics of plot tension in story, theater, and film. Steven Denning (2000) has looked into storytelling from the point of view of communicating in organizations.

Joseph Campbell has identified a story arc that is found across cultures (George Lucas based the original, and massively successful, *Star Wars* film on just this structure). Campbell's simplified version includes the hero's (perhaps reluctantly) accepting an adventure into a different and challenging world; obstacles are overcome and a victory is reached, after which the hero comes back with new powers to benefit self or others. Important points here include a regular change in the hero's fortunes, at times fortuitous and others, treacherous.

Other analyses of writing suggest similar elements. Movies in general have been analyzed as containing three major components: the introduction, the action, and the denouement. Elements include having a setting, characters with flaws as well as (perhaps hidden) talents, a false success before the final success, and a change on the part of the protagonist.

One aspect of drama has been small cycles of tension and release within an overall buildup of tension. Small crises develop along the major theme of the story (see Figure 3-1). This allows the buildup but with some relief along the path (which also allows time for reflection and natural stopping points). This tension is translated to games by the mechanism of adapting the difficulty of the game to put the learner in this sort of tension.

Games as an interactive medium tend to have simplified versions of this thematic complexity. Although there is an ongoing debate about how to meld

Figure 3-1. Story Arc.

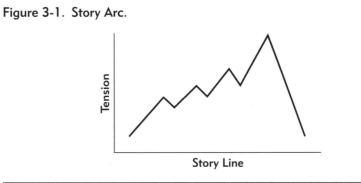

narrative and game play (*ludology,* as the academics would have it), it is recognized that interactive activities are different, and there has been little success in achieving in a game the sort of emotional experience that a good book or film can provide.

The new importance of story in organizations, as people such as Denning (2000) have pointed out, is a realization of the effectiveness of a story to communicate. This comes about by carefully choosing relevant and authentic stories to use, combined with our well-developed cognitive ability to understand stories. Work has gone into identifying the different type of stories necessary to achieve the desired outcome. Key is the ability to use stories that are meaningful to the learner and match the communication goal.

The important elements to abstract from these efforts are the necessity for managing tension (through challenge, in the case of a game) while grounding the action in a meaningful story.

Human-Computer Interaction

In studies of human-computer interaction (HCI) there has been investigation of what makes an effective interactive experience. John Carroll, whose game experience opened Chapter One and whose creation of minimalist instruction was discussed in Chapter Two, noticed that individuals would spend hours learning to play a game but would throw their hands up in frustration at bad task-oriented interfaces. Relevant elements from his list of reflections about what makes games effective include responsiveness, benchmarks, acceptable uncertainty, safe conduct, learning by doing, and control (Carroll, 1982). Responsiveness is feedback from the computer, benchmarks are indicators of outcomes and progress, acceptable uncertainty means that proceeding without complete understanding is okay, safe conduct means that you can make errors and not affect the real world, learning by doing means you must explore, and control means that the learner is the agent of action.

Another area of interest has been the investigation of direct manipulation, the experience of operating on the objects of interest, unmediated by external representations. This experience was manifest for the first time commercially through the game "Pinball Construction Set" by Bill Budge, where players dragged and dropped flippers, bouncers, and so forth onto a backdrop to create a pinball game, which could then be played. Ben Shneiderman (1983) took an initial stab at the components, and then Ed Hutchins, Jim Hollan, and Donald Norman (1986) took another look at this phenomenon. Their take on important elements included a tight coupling between the action one takes at the interface, and the form and speed of the feedback. (I had the good fortune to be studying with Don during this time, and got to not only see the output, but observe the idea development as well, which as we saw in the last chapter was the cognitive annotation that made it a great learning experience!)

Brenda Laurel (1991), from a background in theater, looked at the elements of drama that are important in creating compelling interface experiences. Bruce Tognazzini (1993) looked to another performance medium, the presentation of magic tricks for audiences. Although in a sense these are passive activities for the audience, in another sense they do engage the mind and heart, and both of these folks deliberately looked for the interactive implications. The implications include designing a "flow" of actions so that there is a coherent feeling of an "experience" developed over time, having the outcomes of an action be thematically linked to the action, and having the user experience a perception of frequent opportunities to act from a wide variety of choices.

Game Design

The final area of input is directly from the game design community itself. Several writers have gained reputations for their designs and their reflections on designs. Some have become known almost to the status of legend, whereas others are still practitioners.

Chris Crawford (1990, 2003) has been designing computer games almost as long as there have been computers, certainly from the days of the earliest PCs. Since designing some commercial games, he has undertaken a more philosophical quest, but his reflections remain as some of the most resonant.

Earnest Adams has designed games for many years, and has been eloquent in his reflections and forward thinking about games. His work is often seen in his "The Designer's Notebook" column in Gamasutra, a site for game developers and development (www.gamasutra.com). There are many other authors and relevant papers that are too numerous to review but whose contributions I have scanned through the years to seek further insight. These points influence more the pragmatic issues, which are discussed in Chapter Seven.

The elements that emerge from these writers' musings include the requirement for a balanced level of challenge, the provision of opportunity for exploration, and a theme. Some other ideas include nonlinearity and a variable rate of reinforcement, both of which can be interpreted as a call for some randomness and choice.

David Freeman's new work on emotion in games pushes the underlying concept of broadening and deepening the emotion of the experience (Freeman, 2004). He includes a deep analysis of elements that contribute to an emotionally compelling experience. (He claims to have 1,500 but could only put 300 in the book!) There are a wide variety of specific tips that go into considerable depth on adding emotional attachment to games. It may be more than you need to begin, but as we get serious about creating compelling learning experiences, I'm finding it worth the study.

One of the essentially unique ideas from game design is the concept of level design. Games, while maintaining an overall theme, are divided into levels where you start out, have to get past numerous obstacles and through several different locations, and eventually face a final challenge (often an extra-tough character called a "boss"). Levels may share some skills with other levels and may also introduce or require new ones. Dividing games in these ways gives a bit of the buildup and release of tension found in literature. The levels are, in a sense, mini-games. The overall games are designed for literally hours of playing, so mini-games make sense, but this approach may not be feasible for learning games unless the scope of the skill set being developed is substantial. A game level may be equivalent to one game you are developing.

Synthesis

A review leads me to extract the elements that resonate across the approaches. We have seen common elements that appear in at least a couple of the approaches:

- Thematic coherence
- Clear goal
- Balanced challenge
- Relevance: action to domain
- Relevance: problem to learner
- Choices of action
- Direct manipulation
- Action coupling
- Novel information or events

These elements, in total, provide rich guidance for designing engaging experiences.

Thematic Coherence. Every game is in a genre (or blends several), and the action within the game must be consistent to the theme or model world we develop.

Clear Goal. The player must be presented or discover the goal he or she is trying to achieve within the theme.

Balanced Challenge. An experience that is too simple is not fun, and one that is too difficult is frustrating. As the player improves, the challenge needs to increase appropriately. The tension should relatively wax and wane while maintaining a steady increase.

Relevance: Action to Domain. The dilemmas and consequent decisions that the player makes must be meaningful in the model world.

Relevance: Problem to Learner. The genre of the game and the story line must be of interest to the player.

Choices of Action. There needs to be (at least a perception of) a variety of choices the player can make at any time.

Direct Manipulation. The player should act directly on the model world through the interface.

Action Coupling. Input-output interreferentiality: the action in the world should cause actions that are represented back to the player by consequences in that world.

Novel Information or Events. The play should include elements of chance that make the play nondeterministic.

Summary

The combination of these elements does not provide a prescriptive guarantee of a great game. In addition to ensuring that these elements are balanced and mutually reinforcing (so the interface aesthetics are appropriate for the game setting; for instance, using a medieval script for text in a swords and sorcery title), there is the element of game play. However, using this list as a guideline for development will help ensure that you avoid some major mistakes. Coupled with a systematic design process, there is a great chance of having at least a playable game.

A Play in Three Acts

4

Engagement-Education Synergy

I N THE PREVIOUS TWO CHAPTERS, I developed a list of elements that contribute to learning and engagement, respectively. If you read both lists, it will not be a surprise to see that there is a one-to-one correspondence between elements of the lists. In Table 4-1, the elements from Chapter Two are listed in the Learning column, and the elements from Chapter Three are listed under Engagement. And it is this relationship that suggests the whole is greater than the sum of the parts; aligning engagement and education creates a synergy to make a more compelling and effective experience. Doing good engagement is hard, as is doing good education. Doing both together is even more difficult, but even if the effort is double, the product is more than doubly worthwhile. *Learning can, and should, be hard fun.*

This alignment is the basis for systematically designing games that are both educationally effective and engaging. Although people have been developing "edutainment" for some time in a variety of guises, the lack of

Table 4-1. Initial Alignment.

Learning	Engagement
Contextualized	Thematic coherence
Clear goal	Clear goal
Appropriate challenge	Balanced challenge
Anchored	Relevance: action to domain
Relevant	Relevance: problem to learner
Exploratory	Choices of action
Active manipulation	Direct manipulation
Appropriate feedback	Coupling
Attention-getting	Novel information and events

awareness of this explicit synergy has been a barrier. What we want to do is work through this table and start thinking about what this synergy means for a learning design.

First, we align the elements and choose a term to characterize each in our synergistic model (Table 4-2).

Table 4-2. Synergy and Extracted Terms.

Learning Elements	Engagement Elements	Engaged Learning
Contextualized	Thematic coherence	Theme
Clear goal	Clear goal	Goal
Appropriate challenge	Balanced challenge	Challenge

Table 4-2. Synergy and Extracted Terms, *Continued*.

Learning Elements	Engagement Elements	Engaged Learning
Anchored	Relevance: action to domain	Action-Domain link
Relevant	Relevance: problem to learner	Problem-Learner link
Exploratory	Choices of action	Active
Active manipulation	Direct manipulation	Direct
Appropriate feedback	Coupling	Feedback
Attention-getting	Novel information and events	Affect

From all the learning and engagement terms that could be focused on, getting this list and seeing the alignments isn't obvious. I have been claiming that putting educators and entertainment experts in a room together isn't likely to yield a successful outcome, and I hope this demonstrates why. Those folks do not speak the same language and have no point of common ground. Unless a framework like this is available, there is no real way to allow them to work together.

However, having the alignment gives us a way to start talking about how to design games by finding the common ground and providing a shared language. As demonstrated in the third column of Table 4-2, I'm using the following terms, drawn from both sides in an attempt to provide a neutral balance, in going forward.

Implications

These elements should be systematically examined and the perspectives of the two approaches reconciled. As we're now talking about learning games, I sometimes refer to the recipient of the experience we are designing as the *learner*, but sometimes I'll backslide and refer to the *player*. Although play will be important, unless the instructional objective is ultimately achieved, it will remain something other than a learning experience.

Theme

The game has to have a setting, a context, to create a thematically driven experience. An easy solution is to take advantage of well-known genres, either from literature, movies, or games. The game can be set in the Wild West, in space, or in a medieval setting. It can be a hard-boiled detective story, corporate intrigue, or politics. Whether it takes advantage of a common genre or not, there should be a story, and simplifying and exaggerating real life is definitely an option.

It is important to sweat the details, as we'll talk about in depth in Chapter Six. The interface design, and the story and plot elements need to reinforce the theme. Breaks from the theme will undermine the experience.

In "Quest for Independence" (see Case Study 1, this chapter), the players need to find shelter, food, and money on the streets of a little town. Though grounded in reality, the theme has some exaggerations and simplifications. For instance, the character doesn't have to actually go to work every day; it is assumed on their behalf that they will do that in addition to other actions they take.

Note that it is easy to confuse having an overarching theme with writing a story (that's why I chose *theme* as the label for this element, not *story*). The ideal solution has interactivity, that is, specifically varying consequences of your actions dependent on your choices. Designers familiar with theater or writing can get seduced into linear paths of narrative, with essentially no variation depending on learner actions. Please resist that and fight for interactivity and consequences, unless you are pushed into linearity by outside constraints such as a limited budget or lack of sufficient resources.

Even the feedback can and should come within the theme. If the learner has made an incorrect choice, some consequences in the game world or dialogue from a character make a better feedback mechanism than a non-game intervention. Yes, reflection outside the game and afterward is also likely to be required, but the feedback should be set in the game.

Goal

For the learner to know *how* to choose when presented with decisions (assuming they have the prerequisite knowledge), a goal should be established that is set up in the story. The goal should provide a motivation for the action and a metric for attainment. The easiest situation is if the goal is naturally linked with the theme, such as a theme about a business merger and a goal of reconciling the two company cultures, but that's not a requirement.

From Joseph Campbell we know that there typically is an event that triggers the action in a hero story and therefore in the game. In games there usually is an introduction, a story that sets up the action and lets the player know what their situation is and what the goal is. We also know from Campbell that the goal may change over time—for instance, from merely surviving the onslaught of horrible creatures overrunning our space station to discovering who or what is making them to stopping the authors of the mayhem—and there is a reason for action in a particular direction.

In the case where the goal is not known initially, the goal should be discovered soon, and the story milieu should provide a basis for action. There always needs to be a driver of action. In the case of the detective adventure "Déjà Vu," players awoke with amnesia in a bathroom and had to discover why someone was trying to do them in. Until the exploration proceeded, players had to discover who they were and what they had been doing, at which point they had the final goal of the game, which then involved proving a situation to the satisfaction of the police. In this case, however, they had an initial goal, which then was transformed as the player learned more. Learners need to have a basis upon which to make choices, even if that basis can shift.

Challenge

It's clear from the engagement side that one of the primary elements of a compelling experience is an appropriate challenge, and from the education side that learning similarly happens when problems are pitched at the right level. There needs to be a systematic balance of difficulty that changes as the learner progresses. The challenge in this case arises from the mental task to be accomplished.

Note that low-level objectives, such as being able to recite a piece of knowledge, don't make for particularly interesting games. There are plenty of game "shells" that are available that allow you to put drill and practice in the form of a quiz show or some other window dressing that is not tied to the learning. That is not a particular challenge and is not of interest here; you should reserve the right to make the learning objective more interesting. Although such skills may need to be automated to support further application, they by themselves are not, and should not, be a primary focus but instead an *enabling* component. People seldom need knowledge by itself, but they need to *use* it in some way to accomplish a goal. Place that knowledge in a meaningful context and give yourself a more interesting objective!

In this case, the challenge arises from appropriately applying knowledge to accomplish an important distinction between alternatives. Here the convention is adopted that applying knowledge is a skill, and cognitive skills are what we require as our objectives. Consequently, cognitive skills are what we must test in the game. We will refer to skills as the object of desire in developing our games.

It has been said that boys prefer competitive games whereas girls prefer noncompetitive games. It is my belief that while girls won't typically play the console games, boys will play games that require cognitive effort. Using cognitive challenge instead of motor challenge has, I argue, a broader appeal than any other approach, and allows us to dismiss the gender issue. That said, if you have a single-gender audience, do take advantage of it!

Note that the challenge needs to adapt to the learner. Games typically have levels with associated difficulty. You need to master skills at the lower levels to succeed at the higher levels. In learning, recall you start with limited challenges (through scaffolding) and gradually incorporate more complexity until you can manage the entire task. Similarly, your games should have graduated challenges that shift in measured steps from challenges that your initial audience can handle, but are components of the desired outcome, to the final performance level you need to achieve.

Action-Domain Link

The story and consequent plot twists chosen should be situations where the knowledge really needs to be applied. The action taken by the learner needs to be an application of the knowledge, and one that would make sense in the game world.

A classic bad example was an educational software game where you solved math problems to get more chances to shoot aliens; there was no connection between the math task and the game task. An improvement was where one needed to calculate coordinates to attack menacing sharks (these were early examples, and before the forces of Political Correctness would preclude such themes). You need to find or create a meaningful application of the knowledge to the task.

Note that certain types of skills will more naturally map to particular genres and stories. Although being creative is valuable, not reinventing the wheel is also desirable. Try to avoid clichés, but do try to tap into existing value. It

For a game on project management, where the client had very large construction projects, we moved the setting to terra-forming planets (see Case Study 3 in Chapter Five). Although that's not a real setting in which the clients manage tasks, it is an exaggeration of their situation to another, interesting, context where large-scale project management is needed.

will be a judgment call, but familiar genres can provide leverage to reduce the time learners need to get familiar with the game expectations and interface.

Problem-Learner Link

Another criterion for choosing a theme is that the world and the story within it have to be of interest to the learner. Certain audiences may be more appropriate for certain genres, naturally. In the example about project management, a setting in space was appropriate for the audience of engineers. Such a setting might not be of interest to salespeople, to use a stereotype.

Knowing your audience no longer means understanding what their knowledge is, but also knowing their preferences and attributes as learners. Who they are becomes important, not just what they know. You need to know what gets them up in the morning, and why they're doing this task as opposed to others. You also want to understand the audience's emotional factors, cognitive approaches, and motivations. Recognize that most job or topic categories appeal to particular demographics and that you can and should target the story line to interest those folks.

Criteria may include many of the factors seen on personality profiles. Are they detail-oriented or big picture–oriented? Are they competitive or cooperative? Are they social or solitary? You may also want to know their problem-solving style, systematic or not, and so forth. The more you know about the learners, the better chance you have to design a solution that compels them.

There's another reason for this than just to pick the appropriate setting. Understanding who they are helps you understand the mistakes they make and why. You'll be looking for their mistakes to capture and remediate them, and this information will help you understand why they make the mistakes they make. Learners may make mistakes because they're not trying (which is why the learning should be compelling), but also because of misconceptions they hold. Those misconceptions need to be detected and remediated. As a designer, you will better understand the source of those errors if you know how learners think.

Active

The learner needs to be active in making decisions in the story. Once the story is set up, the learner has to commit to choices and then take action to communicate those choices to the system. The system needs to present consequences of those decisions to the learner and provide further opportunities to act (unless the action is terminal, either successful or unsuccessful).

The choices should be frequent enough to give the learner the experience of being in control. One early game had large sequences of video, after which the character turned to the players and had them make a relatively insignificant choice (to exaggerate: "Should I call them or page them?"), after which the action continued. Time can be sped up or the story line ramped up to ensure frequent choices.

Part of the action is cognitive: the learner needs to be given situations where the decision is complex enough between the alternatives to maintain the challenge. The cognitive activity builds the experience of engagement with the material.

Direct

The learner also has to act to make the choices, and the action required ideally maps to the semantics of the choices. While choosing between options can be done by selecting items from a list, ideally we choose a more direct form of mapping. So, for instance, to choose to move in different directions, we can choose from arrows that point the way, or indicate that it's motion we want (either through clicking on an icon or using a key or mouse button combination) and drag in the appropriate direction.

For another example, if you are choosing between several medications to administer to a patient, it might be better to require choosing from several containers of drugs rather than choosing a text description from a list, particularly if those containers resemble the real ones and discriminating between them is an important skill.

In essence, all interaction is really a form of multiple choices between alternatives. The appearance may be one of continual choice, but at a certain

level it boils down to some finite choices, and we certainly can expect to simplify the world in some sense. This also suggests that, if necessary to meet
pragmatic constraints of schedule or resources, we can resort to simplified
option choices as long as the choices and consequences are meaningful.

To put it another way, if there are conflicts between making a good
action choice and a good cognitive choice, the cognitive wins out. Learners
will forgive the indirect mapping more quickly than a nonengaging story,
and pragmatic constraints may suggest using lower-cost interactions such as
multiple-choice questions to drive the story.

Feedback

Once the choice has been made, the consequences of that choice, in terms of
the story, need to be played out. The decision should have an impact on the
story line, regardless of the choice. That impact should be communicated
back to players in a way that allows them to infer the results of their choice.

The feedback should be staged in the context of the story. That means
that a character in the story, or a change in the world of the story, provides
the feedback. It means *avoiding* having some device or someone external to
the story inform you of the consequences, at least not until the play is done.

For example, the learner, as a salesperson in the story, has chosen to show
the product to the customer before doing sufficient research on the customer's
needs. The consequence should not be external: "That's a bad move, as you
have not yet established with the customer that they have the need your prod-

There is some debate about whether feedback has to come immediately or
whether it can come later. Michael Allen (2002) has argued that feedback
doesn't have to be immediate. The more complex the skill, the more important
the skills, and the closer to the final performance, the more you want learners
to be able to self-monitor. Consider the overall effect, not just the immediate
decision, in deciding on when to make known the full consequences of the
action. However, always do acknowledge that *some* action has occurred.

uct solves." Instead, if you have a rich theme, you might have the customer react negatively and inform you that they don't like "hard sells" and that you don't know their real problem.

The learner's action should have an impact on the story line. Making a choice that gives you feedback but isn't essential to the ongoing action undermines the engagement of the learner in the story. The story should be built around the decisions of the learner, not grafting the decisions onto a story line.

Note that the consequences do not have to occur immediately. Imagine that you have a series of decisions having to do with different cases; for instance, choosing medication. Often you will make many of the choices in the time it takes for one bad decision to percolate through the ramifications (for instance, it may take twenty minutes or more for the effects of overmedication), while other decisions must be made. You can choose to simplify the world, or you can choose to maintain the accuracy, depending on your constraints, but having the decision come back to haunt you later is certainly a plausible outcome in games.

Affect

Finally, the play should not be predictable. Chance should play a role in the action, whether by changing what problems you see or introducing some luck into the ebb and flow of the character's success. There are situations where such variability may not be possible. In such cases, having interesting and dramatic or humorous elements in the story line can help maintain engagement.

Another important element of affect is supporting the theme and mood of the story setting. Having inappropriate dialogue, appearance, or sound effects

I note that Rob Moser (2000) did his Ph.D. with me on the topic of designing games and developing one game concept through to a complete paper prototype, delving deeply into the philosophy of design, the psychology of learning, and the experience of engagement. For in-depth reading, I cannot point you better than to his thesis from the University of New South Wales, Australia.

can undermine the willing suspension of disbelief that is the core of the manufactured experience. For instance, movies and books that are true to a genre are easier to succeed with than ones that bend genres.

Summary

The elements of theme, goal, challenge, action-domain link, problem-learner link, active, direct, feedback, and affect are the factors that lead to engagement and learning. When used synergistically to mutually develop both the engagement and education goals, the whole is greater than the sum of the parts. It is hard to do good education and hard to do good learning, but when you align them, they can mutually support each other.

CASE STUDY 1

"Quest for Independence"
Context

A colleague with connections to the Australian Children's Welfare Agency asked whether I could and would develop a game for them. The agency had an initiative called AfterCare that was concerned with kids who are raised in "Care" (read: without regular parental relationships) and at roughly age eighteen are transitioned out onto the streets. The preparation for this new existence for the kids is idiosyncratic at best. The end result is much homelessness, drug use, and crime.

The AfterCare project was set up to address this problem and had received funding to develop materials. They had produced a comic book, poster, and a video, but they were interested in having a computer game as well, recognizing that the kids would come into the Care centers and play on the computers there. Of course, they had used up their funding but wondered whether I could help them out anyway(!). Serendipitously, I had a stellar student (Dana Kedzier) who was looking for a meaningful project. We took on the challenge.

Constraints

There were several constraints in this process. For one, these kids have low self-esteem. This manifested itself in several ways, including that they were resistant to being told what to do, and also that not succeeding in the game could be damaging. The audience for the game also had low literacy, due to the fact that they often move (or are moved) and consequently have interrupted schooling, and resistance to instruction and lack of role models on the value of learning also doesn't help.

We also had limited access to these kids. They are very much protected (and rightfully so), and the ones who have "graduated" are hard to find. But we did have access to the counselors. And we had two very supportive coordinators working with us.

On the technical side, we had only the old "toaster" Macintosh computers as our environment (only black and white and 512 by 480 screen resolution) and a variety of IBM PCs or equivalents.

Design Process

Since I had taught HyperCard to my interface design class (including Dana) as an environment that allowed focus on design, not programming, and had used HyperCard to develop software including games, we chose that as our development environment. This allowed us to address the Macintoshes but not the PCs.

Design Features

"Quest" provides an example around which we can talk through the elements of engaged learning: theme, goal, challenge, action-domain link, problem-learner link, active, direct, feedback, and affect.

Theme. In this case, our theme was at least partly set for us. We considered using some of the major genres, such as surviving on the streets of a medieval city or a town in the Old West (U.S.), but the challenge of surviving on the streets of a simulated city similar to the ones the kids knew was deemed more appropriate. In wrestling with perspectives—whether in first-person as in many adventure games of the time or in the omniscient top-down third-person view of many role-playing games—we came up with a hybrid that looked angularly down at the characters so we also saw the street they were on. This led us to generate four quarter views of the city, and we subsequently created two separate cities linked by a bus to provide enough variety (which also provided a further occasion to require using money in the game) for all the types of places they needed to visit.

Our initial graphics were not stellar (neither Dana nor I had graphic design experience) but were sufficient to convey the game (see Figure 4-1). Our focus, however, was on the underlying mechanics to implement the "play" of the game. We used icons to help convey the various functions of the locations, due to the learners' low literacy (we figured the word "Care" had an iconic as well as lexical role, and it had no independent graphic icon).

Figure 4-1. "Quest"'s Initial Appearance.

Goal. We talked to the counselors to determine what the learning goals needed to be, and they suggested that these kids needed to learn how to shop and cook. This was not the most promising set of goals for a game (though I was confident we could do it), but fortunately we got a chance to talk to several kids who had graduated and were surviving on their own. They told us that the most challenging task was learning all the "chains" of activity: that to get the government's job-searching allowance, you had to go to a different office to get the form, but then they wouldn't give you the money; you needed a bank account for the money to be deposited in, and to get a bank account you needed references, and to get references you needed some relationships, and so on.

That gave us the main goal of the game: to achieve a secure existence by manipulating the available social system opportunities. We got lots of other ideas for objectives, including the fact that different ethnicities can have different experiences with officials; that your attitude in dealing with an office can affect your success; and that while you're out on the street you have opportunities for sex and drugs, and you have choices about protected or unprotected activities. Only the latter made it in, though players can choose their appearance as one of six characters, and the appearances do characterize variety in ethnicity and gender. Gender actually plays a small role in how you're approached for sexual opportunities.

Challenge. We needed some way to put pressure on the players to be motivated to explore and discover the relationships and contingencies of the social system in the game. To do this in a way that was coherent with the overall goal, we had levels of food and sleep that went down as you moved around, so that there was pressure to obtain money to buy food and a place to live. We provided feedback on this through a set of bars representing the different levels and icons to characterize what each bar was representing.

Due to the low self-esteem of this population, we did not want to go too far in making the game difficult. We put in several levels of play, so that as learners got comfortable they could play a more difficult level (see Figure 4-2). We also put in a small coaching engine that used some very simple rules to help

learners succeed. Research in early exploratory microworlds showed that learners often explored only a small fraction of the available space, yet if they explore thoroughly they're more likely to discover the included underlying relationships. Consequently, our engine looked to see how many moves they'd made and compared that to how much of the world they'd seen. If they had made many moves but hadn't seen a lot, it suggested they explore more thoroughly. It also watched their health levels and suggested the appropriate action if they fell too low. If learners asked for a hint, it would prioritize on these, but if any situation started getting to be game-threatening, it would ask if they wanted a hint. If any of the levels got near game-ending severity, it would present the players with a hint.

Figure 4-2. Adjustable Levels of Challenge.

Action-Domain Link. In this case, we needed learners' actions to affect their success in the game. They could ask for jobs in any of the places, and in the appropriate offices they could ask for forms, purchase identification, and apply for funding or residence. Learners had to explore, but the choices they made gave them feedback (if they asked for a bank account and didn't have enough identification, it would tell them they needed more). If they made the appropriate choice, the consequences would further their success. If not, the consequences could hinder their success.

For example, the kids had the opportunity to obtain condoms and clean needles. Then if offered the opportunity to have sex or do drugs, they could choose to use them or not. Of course, if they didn't have them, they had to choose whether to proceed or not. If they chose to take the risk, the risk was made manifest through a slot-machine metaphor, and they had a probability of catching a disease. The disease they could contract varied, and it included AIDS. They wouldn't die, of course, but could get "too sick to continue" the game.

Problem-Learner Link. The problems in the game were drawn from the concerns and experience of the audience, so we knew that the learners would care about the outcome. We did not try to provide all the answers in the game, however, as part of the goal of the design was to drive learners to the counselors. The realities of finding food and accommodation and money, however, were issues the learners knew they would be facing.

As already mentioned, drugs and sex were part of the game, which provided clear interest for the learners. The alternative locations to visit included video arcades, parks, and other hangouts that reflected the locations they were likely to be interested in. Options in these locations reflected those likely to be really available (for example, food or the ability to ask for a job). There were also some lessons: fancier restaurants used up more of the money for food than others, and fast-food restaurants didn't give so much nutritional value. These weren't explicit but only qualitatively represented in changes in the bars representing money and health.

We also had the ability to use sound, and we did so to emphasize transitions, such as acquiring (or losing) money.

Active. Learners had to explore to discover the available mechanisms to survive and the consequences of actions. Moving around the locations made the health levels change. There were onscreen buttons for hints and help, but they had to be chosen (except in the extreme case).

As mentioned, the learners had to discover the contingencies in the world. They might find a form in an office and take it to the appropriate location but then be told they needed to take other steps (see Figure 4-3).

Figure 4-3. Contingencies.

They could also discover different ways to succeed. They might get money while going to school, or instead choose to take a job and earn money. Experience or a school degree could lead to a better job.

Direct. Given the low literacy of our player audience, we needed to make the interface as direct as possible (see Figure 4-4). To move, there were arrows to indicate where the players might want to move, a bag icon to click to see what they had, and icons for information and hints. Within rooms there could be buttons to press to ask for jobs, buy food, or rent a place. Icons were used with minimal text.

Figure 4-4. Direct Options.

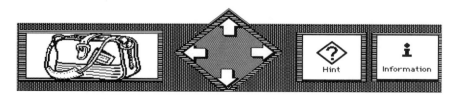

The layout was similarly made direct. There were two major types of locations: locations on the street, where players moved from in front of one building to in front of the next, and locations within buildings. On the street players' options were largely to navigate to other buildings, whereas within the buildings were typically a variety of options depending on the location.

Feedback. The initial form of feedback was, as indicated, the bars indicating players' health levels (see Figure 4-5). These would change depending on actions taken, such as actions that required money or served as sustenance or rest.

Figure 4-5. Graphic Feedback.

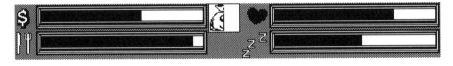

A second form of feedback was the auditory feedback that accompanied most of these changes. As indicated, there were cash register sounds for money changing hands, increasing tones for health and food going up, and decreasing tones for levels going down.

Certain types of actions happened under the game engine's control, such as beneficially receiving money or not-so-beneficially losing money. These actions were signified by dialogue boxes, which indicated the event. Some actions required choices by the learner, such as choosing to have unprotected sex. These choices were also mediated by dialogue boxes, and the consequences were made clear in the same mode.

Affect. The opportunities to have sex or do drugs, as well as events that enhanced or diminished levels such as the player's financial reserves, were probabilistic, meaning that they happened at random times but with a certain average frequency (see Figure 4-6). This kept the game from being deterministic and enhanced the game play.

Figure 4-6. Unpredictable Events.

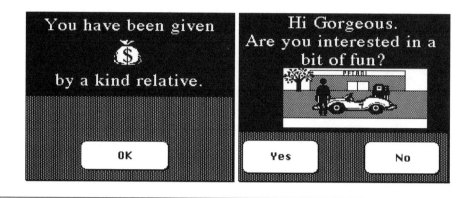

A second factor that enhanced the appeal came as an outcome of the first version. The folks we were working with from the AfterCare project and the agency were thrilled with the game play but not with the admittedly basic graphics. I assisted them in approaching a philanthropic agency that provided funding to develop the graphics further. In addition to a graphic design agency, the kids themselves got a chance to contribute to the graphics. The result was a superior appearance (see Figure 4-7).

Outcomes

During the development process, after refining the game play through testing it ourselves, we wanted to test it on our audience. We were fortunate to get the two youths who had initially helped us by allowing us to interview them (we felt giving them a chance to play the game was a reward for having helped us develop it). It was interesting that the challenge was such that the first player did not succeed at the game. Another who had watched the first, however, and had a chance to focus on strategy (the first had to try to master the strategy while also manipulating the interface, a common problem for learners) was successful, thus demonstrating a benefit of working in pairs. A

CASE STUDY 1, *Continued*

Figure 4-7. Improved Graphic Appearance.

third youth had watched the second and succeeded as well. We were gratified to watch the first player demand a chance to play again and succeed.

A cautionary note: The funding that developed the graphics also funded the development of the game for PCs. Against my recommendations, they allowed the developer to choose the environment to develop in, and the environment chosen did not use the same programming metaphor as HyperCard (it would've been a relatively straightforward task in another extant tool that did share the same metaphor). The PC version ended up being buggy.

Also, on the Macintosh version, the graphics folks moved some of the buildings around and in doing so broke some of the code. I had to cram many hours on evenings and weekends in the course of a few weeks to fix the code in time for the launch. The lesson learned is to choose your development environment carefully and ensure that any work done is done with a full understanding of the mechanics, or allow time to accommodate impacts on the total integration.

The resulting game was launched at a party celebrating the entire line of AfterCare project products and was in steady use in Care centers thereafter. It was also featured on a science TV program in Australia. A subsequent student project ported the game to run on the Web, as proof of the concept that such interactive activities can be Internet-delivered.

On a personal note, this was one of the most rewarding projects I've worked on, as it was an intriguing design challenge and it really helped an important social need. I think that there are lots of ways in which games could meet important needs (we prototyped a subsequent game that helped kids talk about and document difficult issues in their life). Anyone want to play?

5

Trajectory

WE HAVE SEEN that we can align elements of engagement with learning to achieve a more successful learning experience. How does that play out in designing actual learning experiences? In this chapter we will examine a trajectory of solution templates from enhanced ISD through scenarios to a full game engine. We will see examples to illustrate these various approaches. In the next chapter we will talk about a design process that can get us from go to whoa.

The underlying principle is that we want to change practice from the ubiquitous multiple-choice question, under any of its guises, into a decision point in a story. And, yes, these *can* be phrased in the form of a multiple-choice question, for in truth all decisions (with the possible exception of human fine or coarse motor control) are essentially a choice among a number of alternatives. Although it might be argued that even an apparently continuous range of motion really can be quantized, I won't do that here. Instead, I'll simply suggest that for the broad range of learning objectives we want to address, we can quantize the choices and make the decision to be one of multiple choices (even if it appears to be a continuous variable under manipulation).

We want to ensure that the responses by learners require the application of knowledge to make decisions. We want to frame our learning objectives to require using knowledge to make decisions, and then embed those decisions into a context. Several principles are important here. We want to ensure that we are applying the knowledge, not just testing to see whether it is present. We want to make sure that the knowledge is contextualized in a setting that is meaningful to the learner, who then exercises the knowledge in the way it will be exercised outside the learning experience, and we would like the feedback to come from within the story.

I characterize five levels of increasing engagement and effectiveness in applying this principle to the design of e-learning:

- Level 0: Enhanced ISD
- Level 1: Mini-Scenarios
- Level 2: Linked Scenarios
- Level 3: Contingent Scenarios
- Level 4: The Full Monty

These levels provide us with intermediate steps of increasing engagement and effectiveness that may be required under pragmatic constraints. Note that these levels are not fixed but form a useful scheme through which to think about ways to approach engagement in manageable steps. They do reflect, to some extent at least, how things actually are developed. On one project I worked with a client (see Case Study 3, this chapter), we developed a project at level 2 and pleased their client so much we were next engaged to develop a full game (level 4)!

We have seen in Chapter Two that an enhanced instructional design incorporates a more motivating introduction, multiply represented concepts, cognitively annotated examples, scaffolded practice, and guided reflection. Consequently, here I elaborate on the four levels above the base level. We now want to more closely examine the practice element (the role for games). In addition to ensuring that we are requiring knowledge application, we are going to aim toward placing the choices in context, aligning response mechanism to cognitive operation, and framing feedback in context.

Level 1: Mini-Scenarios

In *mini-scenarios* we follow traditional instructional design, but we then couch our practice items in contextual language. (Yes, this really is what we should be doing in enhanced ISD, but it's worth pulling out for extra focus here.) We still have our traditional introduction (here suggesting a cartoon), concept (with re-representation), and examples (perhaps a story), and then we create contexts for the decisions so that there is a theme that sets the stage for the choice (Figure 5-1). So for the practice, there is a setup of the context, an

Figure 5-1. Mini-Scenarios.

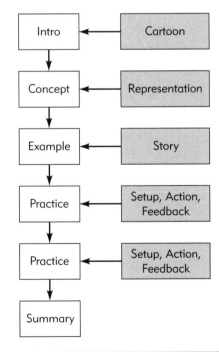

action taken by the learner, and feedback, all set within the context. This context only surrounds the individual decision, but it is an improvement over knowledge test questions.

I will talk more about how to systematically design such a story in the next chapter, so here I merely emphasize the scope of the story in this scenario. The point here is that the easiest and first move is to take your standard practice elements and at least make each one of those a scenario.

Let's take a sample and work through it. When I taught interface-interaction design, I might have asked a question such as

What are the four stages of the design process cycle?

A. Analysis, design, implementation, delivery

B. Design, implementation, evaluation, delivery

C. Analysis, specification, implementation, evaluation

D. Requirements, specification, implementation, evaluation

As I had design projects to test the students' ability to execute, and for other reasons, I probably did ask such rote questions (as hard as it is to now admit it; for the answer, please see Chapter Six). Now to make this a mini-scenario, I have to think of a situation in which a designer might need to specify the stages of the design process. It would have to be a situation in which you have to establish credibility (answering such a question, instead of actually doing it) with a client, perhaps, or your team. It could be at the planning or selling stage of a project, and a designer might have created four project-plan graphics (for a presentation, say) with the above labels. Then the client could not select you for the project if you can't even get the order correct. Or an assistant might have dropped the labels when moving a chart to a new project room and asks you to rearrange them (the principle of directness suggests grabbing the appropriate ones from a pile and dropping them in order). Then you might lose your team if you can't even organize the labels correctly.

Of course, I would be more likely to frame the whole question differently. This still is more a knowledge test than a knowledge application. To change that, it would be more typical to have to recognize when it is time to transition between stages of design and where to go (and, perhaps, to have pressure to do something else). So, for example, I might have a problem where a manager comes and says something along the lines of, "I see you've got a working design, excellent work. Time to move on to the Acme project that's already late." You'd have to choose a reply from a list such as,

"Great. I'm looking forward to a new challenge."

"It's just a prototype. I need to remain on this project until engineering delivers the final product."

"I was going to take a bit longer to verify we'd met our design goals."

One advantage to this approach is that it makes it easy to create vastly disparate contexts that cover the space of application, thus supporting the transfer that is one of our learning goals. Typically, unless we're training a very specific skill, there are more settings in which the skill application is appropriate than we can model.

One of the things that scares designers is to not test the knowledge and ensure that it is known. However, the claim here is that we can make the situation require the knowledge in an unambiguous way, and that requiring the knowledge in a meaningful way ensures that the learner is motivated to acquire it. Van Merriënboer (1997) is concerned about the component knowledge and the cognitive skills that surround the knowledge to apply it. He suggests that the knowledge be practiced until mastered, but he prefers that it occur within the context of applying the skill. This is, to me, an essential element: having an environment in which the learner is compelled to want to learn the knowledge.

The problem with mini-scenarios is that the story line is unlikely to be sufficient to engage the learner in more than a superficial way. Although knowledge application is better than a traditional question, the persistence of the story does not percolate along, and we find it essentially impossible to include the element of novelty. We will need to take another step to do better.

"MediaSpeak"

A number of years ago I was working with a new media firm, Access Australia Cooperative Multimedia Centre, which was approached by the principals of Media Skills, a firm that taught people how to deal with the media. Public speaking is one of the biggest fears many people have, and talking to the media is a facet of that form of performance. Consequently, the two founders of Media Skills had developed a unique approach to this training and offered it around the country. They were at the stage in their business when a book would have made sense, but they wanted to do something different and were asking us about doing something new.

Access was an Australian government–sponsored initiative tasked with developing Australian multimedia and Internet capability. We were looking at putting a course online as the first effort in a move to explore online learning as a corporate strategy, and this seemed like an opportune project, so off we went.

Context

Access's approach was well developed. They ran workshops in which people went through their frameworks and practice exercises, and the class ended up with the attendees being filmed in an interview with journalists whom the principals knew.

The materials were in a workbook that was deliberately incomplete, so people who paid could fill in the missing bits as active learning, but anyone with the book who were not taking the course would have difficulty inferring what the key points were.

As we were looking at the course as a potential revenue operation, we also wanted a user experience that would be commercially viable. Consequently, there was pressure to ensure that the overall design was aesthetically appealing, as well as educationally effective.

The principals had quite high demand for their course, so they had little time to work with us. They had had considerable trouble meeting the demand, particularly in rural areas where they could not get enough people at one event to justify holding the course. This situation made the online course quite appealing.

Constraints

One of the constraints we had at the time was that the network infrastructure to reach the rural areas was still fairly limited, so bandwidth was an issue. Also, the principals wanted to use media clips to illustrate their points, and rightly so, but that even more seriously proscribed any other uses of media. This was potentially in conflict with the goal of creating a highly engaging experience.

Though I had already conducted a fair amount of research into what makes experiences engaging (in addition to my learning and instruction background), we also had available an experienced producer, Jan Zwar, who had guided the development of several CD-ROMs of commercial quality. Consequently, we decided that she would take the lead on the engagement side, and I would be responsible for the educational design, thus allowing a creative tension to generate the best output. This worked for several reasons, one being that I had developed my framework enough so that we could communicate, and the second being that she was professional and organized but also thoughtful, good-natured, and fun.

We had some constraints on our resources, but we also had a budget. As our organization was a consortium of new media companies and universities, a competitive bidding process led us to choose to use the media resources of one of our university partners for production.

Design Process

The work started with my going through their workshop workbook and developing an understanding of the content. We then needed to create an outline of the content components, what I call a *content model* or content architecture. This is the breakup into components identified in Chapter Two:

concept, examples, practice, and reflection. (It was from these principals, by the way, and their trick of suggesting to their students to practice the statement formula on their children, that I was shown the value of supporting learners in keeping the knowledge active in the time between learning and real practice.)

We decided to make the different components available directly to learners through labels, so those who were self-directed learners could take control of their learning experience (see Figure 5-2). We used dotted lines (follow the bouncing ball) to indicate the path for learners who might want guidance in navigating through the content. Anecdotal reports from the producer (I had returned to the United States for family reasons before the production was finished) suggested that about half the audience took the safe path, but the other half took advantage of the navigational capabilities. This was an initial attempt at, and strong support for the concept of, supporting different learner styles. UNext, an online university offering courses developed by faculty members from known institutions, independently ended up adopting a similar navigation structure for its commercial courses. (It was subsequently the basis of an intelligently adaptive learning system, but that's another story.)

Figure 5-2. Instructional Component–Based Navigation.

Source: Media Skills Pty. Ltd. Reprinted with permission.

We were concerned about the right granularity to use, and ended up breaking the content into three main modules around the three major frameworks they had: understanding the media's life so as to be better able to know what increases the likelihood of them taking your statement, framing a good media quote according to the principals' formula, and working with media questions to get your statement across.

From that content structure, I used the workbook to draft initial prose and practice items. For practice, we took the notion of scaffolding very seriously and took care to provide a graduated series of practice items to develop confidence and skill slowly for an area that causes such anxiety.

We developed very simple practice tasks initially, such as identifying the components of a well-framed comment (see Figure 5-3) or sorting out well-formed from ill-formed media quotes. We subsequently had them choose the best comment from a set, and then gave them circumstances to create their own responses. These could not be automatically marked by technology at the time (and at the time of writing this is still largely an impractical approach), but we developed a notion of providing model answers (which I would now also supplement with guidance about how to evaluate your own response). I believe this is an important opportunity, as to the extent that the learner internalizes the self-evaluation, the learner becomes self-improving (another concept from cognitive apprenticeship).

The intended final practice was an interview with a journalist, which was beyond our capability, but it is a big jump between answering text questions with no time pressure and answering live to a journalist's interview prompts. We came up with the concept of using a digital answering machine, which could be programmed to read a question and record the response. The response could be replayed, as could a model response. To get to the correct question, the user would navigate a menu through the use of numbers (first press a 3, then a 2 . . .). We created a cover story that the system was the phone menu for a news agency, with print, television, and radio divisions and different journalists within each division, so we could take the learner

CASE STUDY 2, *Continued*

Figure 5-3. Initial Mini-Scenarios.

Exercise 1

Identify the "A" response in (a) - (c) below. Then identify
the <u>bridge</u> by nominating either the bridging word used
(eg "and", "but") or identifying it as a "silent" bridge.

Example:

Q: "How much of a setback to the project is this?"
A: "We're actually treating it more as a test for the
project and it's proving valuable in many ways. It's like
crash-testing a car before you put it in the car yards. At
least you know where the weak spots are and can fix
them."

> **A = Address**
> (the issue of the question is: how will the project be
> affected?)
>
> **Bridge =** "and"

(a) "Can you confirm that chemical sprays have
contaminated the river?"

"I can only go on what we know so far, and that is there *is*
some contamination. But, as for what caused it - we're
testing samples, talking to neighbours, and looking at a
whole lot of different options. We'll let *you* know as soon
as *we* know."

⚪ Answer   ⚪ Acknowledge
⚪ Address   ⚪ Attempt

| Bridge... ▾ |

Source: Media Skills Pty. Ltd. Reprinted with permission.

to different questions by indicating that the reporter you needed to talk to
was so-and-so of the X division. Thus, learners would find a practice item
that directed them to call a number and choose the print division, say, and
then choose a specific journalist, who would ask them questions and then
pause for their answer. We provided a cover story and necessary information
on the Web site (so they could practice as we advised them to do for real).
This provided a valuable extra step between asynchronous text and synchro-
nous live communication.

CASE STUDY 2, *Continued*

In the course of developing the prose for the project, I received an object lesson in writing that has stuck with me since (also see Chapter Seven). Jan was looking for ways to enhance the content, and one of the steps she took was to hire a writer of comedy skits for television. It was disheartening to have this writer take a paragraph of my carefully crafted prose and reduce it to two sentences, reliably and repeatedly. I did have to change a word here and there, to return the meaning of a phrase, but overall it was an elegant job. I like to think that I have learned from the experience, and find that I can similarly reduce much prose authored by designers by a factor of 20 to 40 percent. (Including my own first drafts.)

One other outcome of our process was the use of cartoons (see Figure 5-4, as well as Chapter Seven). We wanted a lively, colorful appearance, but we did not have the resources for much in the way of photos or media. We experimented with cartoons, trying out several designers, and found them to work very well. They met the aesthetic appeal my partner was looking for, the educational value I wanted, and yet were quite parsimonious with bandwidth. We used them to help the audience understand why this content was important, with some humorous illustrations of the importance of accurate communication. We also used them for examples, where I found that they both

Figure 5-4. Instructional Cartoons.

News is all about NOW. As they say, yesterday's news is today's fish 'n' chips wrapper.

Source: Media Skills Pty. Ltd. Reprinted with permission.

CASE STUDY 2, *Continued*

communicated well with our intended audience and had the additional value that we could use "thought bubbles" to communicate the underlying thought processes of the characters working through the necessary steps.

We gave the production team the prose, the graphics, and the practice questions, and they put together the content that we reviewed, refined, and finalized.

I'm not covering here some of the technical discussions about mechanisms to check and record outcomes of practice and other details of this content, which were done long enough ago that any solutions would require an assessment of new technologies.

Outcomes

The project was in one sense a success and in another (and more serious way) it was unsuccessful. On the one hand, the content was well received by audiences and won some awards for design (see Figure 5-5). On the other hand,

Figure 5-5. Media Skills Content.

Source: Media Skills Pty. Ltd. Reprinted with permission.

the business model that surrounded it was ultimately not viable (too far ahead of its time, for one thing), and it never became a commercial success.

The lessons learned, however, were of tremendous value in helping me practice and refine the concepts about how to meld engagement and learning.

Level 2: Linked Scenarios

Linked scenarios set a series of decisions into one overarching story line (Figure 5-6). Decisions get sequenced into longer story lines. Each of the game problems are set in the same theme. Given that most learning is about processes that are more complex than a simple decision, this naturally maps to the type of skills we need to develop.

Figure 5-6. Linked Scenarios.

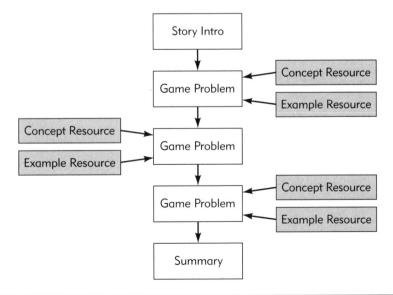

In another change, we don't necessarily have to bring in the content and examples before we launch learners into the scenario. We can instead make information resources that contain the content for a particular decision, and examples, available directly from the decision situation, as illustrated. Ideally, we place the resources into the story line, as well. The examples, for instance, might be stories from a character in the thematic world, and the reference tool used on the job is the one available within the situation. We can also provide links to external resources in the game context. We can, of course, retain the traditional structure of content and examples before the practice, but we subvert the potential to motivate learners from the situations to be interested in the content.

It is slightly harder to write linked scenarios, since you need to maintain a story line over more decisions, but the benefits are substantial. By creating an overarching story, we get enhancements for both engagement and learning. First, we can take the time to create a more compelling experience. We can create characters who can grow or change over time, and we can ramp up the tension across the decisions. We also can connect the sequences of activities that occur together, giving a more complex practice opportunity, and help develop the relationships between components of the learning goal.

One of the potential concerns is that linking decisions into one story line might not provide enough breadth to support transfer. When you're looking at a process that has broad transfer, however, there are several ways to get around this. For one, you can and should create several scenarios for the process, each set in a different setting. So if the content is talking to the media, you could have one instance of talking with a television crew around a polluted river and another time talking on radio about a new product announcement. Alternatively, you can build a variety of situations into one story line, where you have to do the same task in several different mini-contexts. So, for example, you might have to handle two media situations as the media spokesperson for ACME International, one dealing with announcing a new product, the other dealing with a business mistake.

These scenarios, however, need to carry on to the next decision regardless of how the learner performs. There may be consequences in the feedback, but some agent needs to make things okay again, so that you can proceed to the next stage of the decision. If you made too great a mistake in a variety of procedures, you would not be able to continue, but in this model you do proceed (or it doesn't qualify). So to maintain the story, you typically have some agent (boss, robot, angel, for instance) catch the mistake, give you feedback, and then fix your error so you can continue. From the point of view of exploratory learning, however, this is not so desirable as having to actually accept the consequences, and see how things play out.

Project Management Overview, Phase 1

Vis-a-Vis, a media development house, came to me with a project on teaching project management to non-project managers. Their client was a state agency that conducted large construction projects. In this case, large means millions of dollars and an average of about five years per project. The goal was to develop content that was a significant step beyond traditional instructional design.

Context

My client on this project had significant strengths in graphic design, animation, and digital storytelling. What they did not possess was experience in learning theory design or a real understanding of the nature of interactive design. My role was to provide the design, which they would produce. Their graphic forté, as illustrated in prior work, was fantastic creatures and settings, including a book of the imaginary fauna of a planet that had been introduced to the general population through *Star Wars*.

Their client had moved to add a matrixed structure of project managers working across the traditional engineering teams to deliver their large projects. Several main categories of engineers had been responsible for tasks along the major phases of a project, but there had been handoff, with no one group necessarily owning the project from concept to completion. The concern was first that the engineers might not understand the value provided by the project managers, so an objective for this content was to develop their understanding of the project management process. We also wanted to give the engineers an understanding of why the project managers have so much power and how much pressure they are under. Consequently, there was a subgoal of helping the engineers understand that this is not necessarily a job for all and that they should be glad that someone else had to handle these tasks. The content was also intended as a way to help potential project managers see if this was a task they might enjoy.

As a subtext, engineers were not necessarily aware of their role in the successful execution of a project. The main task of engineers is to deliver accurate and timely estimates and plans. Engineers do not necessarily understand the ramifications of an error in data or a lapse in schedule. A second, related, theme was the awareness that some individuals can be difficult to work with, and by exposing the engineers to these issues, they might appreciate the need to be cooperative partners in the work process.

Constraints

One of the constraints was that the content, while supposedly pushing the envelope, had to pass muster with the supervisor of the actual owner of the process within the client organization. That meant that although we needed to take the content to a new level, we could not go so far as we wanted. Essentially, there had to be identifiable components of traditional instructional design.

There existed rich material about the project management process in the form of their *Project Management Book of Knowledge* modeled on one by the Project Management Institute and adapted for the organization's processes. Naturally, as so often happens, the expectation was that the content would be rewritten as e-learning. (This is a process I argue against, suggesting instead that learning situations drive learners to the content.)

The production team was overseas, and consequently another constraint was the lack of tight coupling between design and production. However, I had a great project manager (and talented audio engineer), Jason Shaeffer, who managed the schedule and budget and helped ensure an effective flow of communication.

Design Process

The first element of the design was actually determining the objectives. The objectives identified above came out of an extensive process of data gathering, not from the work as stated in the initial contract. The proposal that my client had presented me did not accurately reflect the real needs for the content, and it took considerable work talking with different stakeholders to identify the real objectives. This was not surprising, as the learning side was not the area of expertise of my client, but it did create some extra work and consequent stress on the timeline.

I was adamantly against rewriting the content of the project management book to go online, and I wanted to put the learner into a situation where they had to make appropriate (but high-level) project management decisions. This included making decisions about what to do when projects go wrong and how to deal with difficult people. The other people the project manager needed to work with included project engineers and stakeholders. Since the player wouldn't necessarily have knowledge of project management, I proposed that the player would control a character who was a new project manager and would have to make the decisions for the character.

As my client had specific expertise in fantastic settings, the audience was engineers, and the type of projects were medium to large construction, I chose a science-fiction setting and made the task to be terra-forming planets. This played to the strengths of the production team, appealed to the audience, and exaggerated the tasks in an interesting way but mapped fairly directly back to the real setting. The character would start as a new hire in the terra-forming division, inheriting the projects of a mysteriously departed previous project manager. Some light touches were added, including an initial hype-ridden recruiting poster that did not map well to the reality of a bureaucratic office.

A consideration was to believably simplify the task to support the learner. To do so, an "intelligent" agent in the form of a portable device was added, and this agent would handle low-level details and allow the player to make the important decisions. This device could provide access to reference materials as well. A boss was added to set the stage initially through a welcome speech and to monitor the player's performance. As the scope did not allow for any more than linear content, the boss would also step in and fix any mistakes the player made.

The content was broken up into three major chunks, and each played out over a "day" of the character's time. Different bits of information were made available to the learner, such as newscasts to set the context for a change such as a new stakeholder, and stories about previous projects that would assist the learner in understanding the feedback (see Figure 5-7).

Figure 5-7. Linear Story Board.

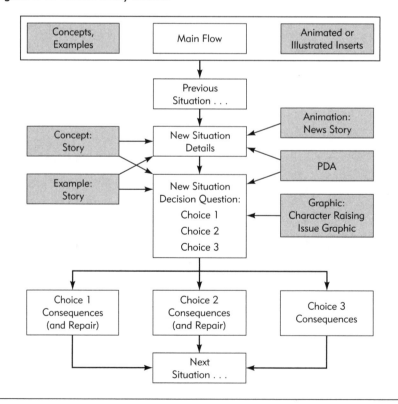

This sample story board shows the main path of the narrative in the middle, where you have a decision, and several responses designed to capture misconceptions about how to deal with it. If you chose correctly, you'd get kudos in the story. If you didn't choose correctly, somehow it would be made okay, usually by your boss. Available from the main story line were examples and concepts, both in the case available as stories (at other times they might be available as information resources available from your intelligent agent). There were also "events" that used news stories and other means to help move the story along, and for production purposes we indicated when a particular graphic was needed. The real story board would have actual content or pointers thereto.

Over my objections, a portion of the underlying concept was actually recited by a character as a monologue. I prefer to have the story line drive people to the material, but it was deemed that this material needed to be in the content, even though it was already available in the *Project Management Book of Knowledge.* In general, however, we did not use the content to present concepts but to challenge the learner and motivate them to access the relevant knowledge.

The content was developed in Flash, with decisions being made by the character, and animations and dialogue conveying the flow of the game. Links would bring up the associated elements as the learner determined. The final solution was hosted on a learning management system (LMS). The resulting look had alien characters, a space setting, a personal digital assistant (PDA) for content, and a place for the game story line. Figure 5-8 shows a fleshed out wire frame, sans content, that was used to validate the look and feel for the client.

Figure 5-8. Graphic Elements of Screen Interface.

Outcomes

The resulting scenario was deemed successful, so much so that my client was given the opportunity to develop a full game. The challenge was that the game had to cover the same content that had already been covered, without being redundant. I again was granted responsibility for the design, and we ended up creating a game that required practicing the knowledge. But that's another story.

Level 3: Contingent Scenarios

The next level is the creation of *contingent scenarios,* or branching scenarios, where now your choices do have consequences, and what you see is contingent upon what choices you make (Figure 5-9). Learners can make mistakes and experience the consequences of those mistakes but also take steps to recover, a scenario closer to how things work in the real world. As with linked scenarios, the examples and concepts are ideally made available from the story line, though they can also be presented before.

Figure 5-9. Contingent Scenarios.

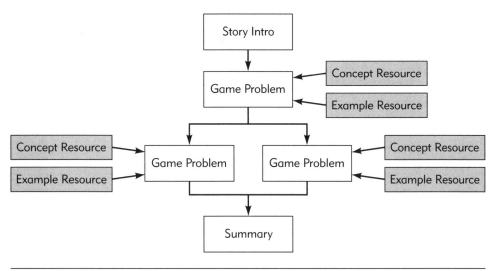

The key to choosing the appropriate alternate paths comes not from making believable alternatives—though those can play a role when better alternatives are exhausted—but from the misconceptions learners have demonstrated when applying the knowledge. The more likely the misconception is to be exhibited by learners, the more important it is that that option be made available and trapped.

It is considerably more work to write contingent scenarios, as you have to develop several different paths through the material and keep track of all options. The more paths made available, the better the learner experience, but the bookkeeping overhead goes up similarly. Developing and keeping track of alternate paths grows exponentially with the number of options. One of the tricks used in computer games, and recommended, is to have the paths converge on certain points so that you do not have infinite branching but have several ways to get to the same point.

There are powerful advantages to the contingent model, in that the learner can replay the scenario several times, exploring alternate paths not chosen in previous uses. This moves us much closer to the goal of an exploratory environment.

The downside is that the exploration stops when all paths have been explored. There are only a limited, "hand-knit" variety of paths available. An ideal would be to have new situations generated on the fly, creating an essentially infinite variety of situations. In short, to move from hand-crafted scenarios to situations generated from a full game engine.

CASE STUDY 4

Vehicle Selling

My client in this case was Knowledge Anywhere, an e-learning solutions provider who specializes in custom-content delivery on a tight budget and schedule. They do this through excellent project management. I had worked with them for over a year when we tackled this project.

Context

They had a client who manufactures large transportation vehicles and is positioned as the quality maker of these vehicles. Their concern was that their sales force was used to "product selling," using traditional sales tactics.

The client had heard about the "solution selling" approach whereby sales folks do research to identify what customer problems are and only then talk to the customer to ensure that the product will actually meet the customer's needs.

The vehicles have hundreds of features, and showing them all can take more than the standard twenty minutes available to demonstrate a product to a customer. The task is to do the research necessary to determine which of the features should be shown to ensure that the customer sees that the vehicle is a viable solution.

Knowledge Anywhere's manager of project managers, Doug Wieringa, had responsibility for this project (he also manages projects) and was looking for ideas to enhance the practice.

Constraints

The first constraint was the audience. Sales folks are rewarded for closing sales. Thus, they want to spend time talking to customers, trying to close deals. They do not want to take time to learn something new. That's time away from making calls, and they know that calls are what increase the likelihood of closing a deal. We needed an activity that they could understand was valuable.

A second constraint was budget. The content budget had a small amount for practice activities, and that was all that was available to use. Whatever we did had to come very cheaply.

Design Process

With this challenge, it seemed plausible that putting the learners into a tough vehicle-selling scenario that had lots of opportunities to go wrong would work. It couldn't be a linear scenario, as the learners had to have some way to recognize that they had got it wrong. It needed to be exploratory and challenging. We certainly didn't have the resources for an underlying engine, but we felt we could manage a branching story line.

The goal was to lure the player into making the wrong choice, and as a consequence not get to see the data that would result from actually choosing to do research. We originally wanted to have a score that depended on how good a choice they made in order to tap into sales folks' natural competitiveness, but with the budget we didn't have the capability to track a score across the content. Instead, we designed a quiz at the end that queried players about what they should show, and this could be scored. The information about what to show was to be gradually revealed as the player successfully navigated the scenario. Wrong choices terminated early, leaving the player with insufficient data to do well on the subsequent quiz.

We were concerned that the scenario had to be plausible. It was critical that we had a believable individual to sell to. Fortunately, Doug is not only a great project manager and project manager mentor, but also his background is in writing. Together we developed a story line, and he wrote the script, based upon his research, to develop the original content.

The implementation used HTML pages for the nodes of the story, hard-coded links to implement the scenario's branches, and an existing tool to score the quiz. The resulting flow provided a long interaction for the right choices but a short path for the wrong ones (see Figure 5-10).

The actual scenario had text, dialogue, and stock photos—nothing spectacular. Good writing on Doug's part made the events that drove the story plausible and the dialogue believable. All the rest was just choosing the branches.

Figure 5-10. Flow Diagram(s) for Scenario.

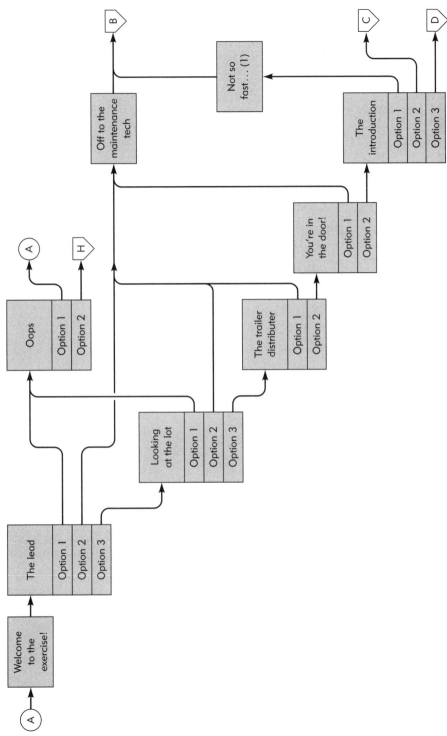

Figure 5-10. Flow Diagram(s) for Scenario, *Continued.*

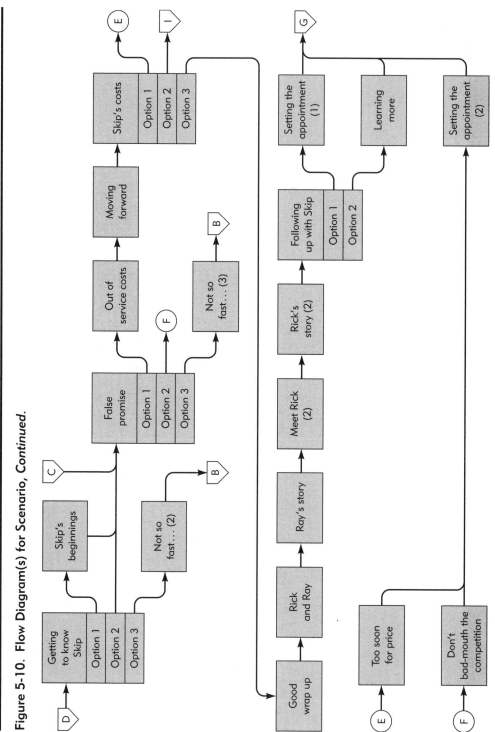

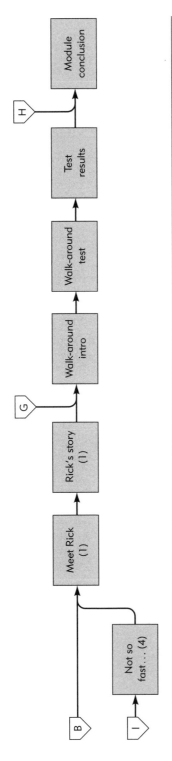

Source: Knowledge Anywhere, Bellevue, Washington. Reprinted by permission.

Outcomes

The anecdotal evidence is that the scenario was a hit. We have quotes from players about how they were challenged and learned from the content.

We have subsequently used scenarios elsewhere and justified the cost of a scenario engine to make it easier to create these in the future.

Level 4: The Full Monty

The full game approach is to build an engine that drives the game from an underlying model that serves up activities by rule, probabilities, and variables, not from a hard-wired structure (Figure 5-11). A world model provides the theme, which wraps around practice activities, which are driven from an engine. Concepts and examples can be embedded or linked externally. In this case you motivate attention to concepts and examples from within the game. You can also take the more traditional presentation of the information (concepts, examples) before engagement in a game or, of course, mix them.

Figure 5-11. Full Game Model.

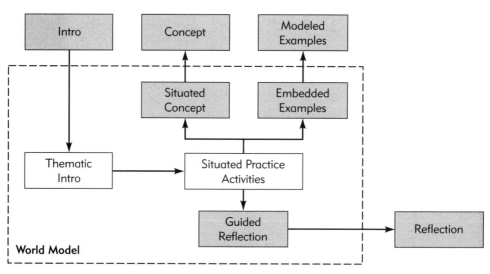

Games with embedded resources are one key to the future of learning. When we can't adequately provide real practice with support, such contextualized practice mimics and consequently maximizes transfer to the situations where the knowledge will actually be applied.

Having a full game engine is the ideal situation for achieving learning outcomes. The notion is to have this underlying engine use a set of rules and probabilities to create decision opportunities on the fly. This engine is initialized with values, after which the player's actions have consequences in terms of changes to values that are processed by rules to see what new situation arises. Then conditions are checked to see what the next decision to present to the player should be. The point is to have a dynamic determination of the decision to present to the learner, based upon rules. We also have some probabilities in there that keep the action from being completely deterministic. We can calculate the outcome of the learner's actions and use that, along with some random outcomes, to determine what happens next.

Simulations

Having a full game engine is very much like what most people call simulations. Simulations use underlying models, qualitative or quantitative, to describe the state of a situation and the consequence of changes. These models use variables and equations or rules to capture relationships between them. Simulations become interactive if there are mechanisms to alter the settings of variables in the model and outputs to represent the state of the system. A person can manipulate the simulation and explore the relationships by observing changes in the situation.

Giving people initial states of the model and goals to achieve turns the simulation into a scenario. A scenario can become a practice exercise if there are goals established for the exploration that require the successful application of some knowledge to achieve. And it becomes part of a learning exercise if there are components such as concepts, examples, and reflection surrounding the practice.

What separates games from scenarios is adjusting the challenge to create an experience of flow, where the challenge is managed and tuned to *pull* the learner through the learning. With the right mix and settings of tension and other elements, a scenario becomes a game, whether the characteristics were established deliberately or accidentally. As mentioned earlier, Microsoft "Flight Simulator" was not intended to be a game, at least initially. Of course, the flip side is that a game can be merely a scenario (or worse) if the elements are not aligned to achieve engagement.

One of the benefits of having an underlying model is that you can add some random elements (tuned properly, as we'll see later) to ensure that the outcome is *nondeterministic,* that is, that the outcome is never fixed. Although you shouldn't mess with the underlying model of a domain, you can introduce events that affect the situation. This is important, as it provides replay, since even with the same decisions the outcome is not completely pre-ordained. With replay, learners can continue to develop their skills to their own level of comfort. Some learners will advance quickly and need more difficulty faster, whereas others may take longer to advance. One design really can't accommodate all the variation you can experience as well as have a flexible implementation, and an underlying engine can assist here.

Another benefit to using an underlying engine is that you can adjust the challenge to the learner on the fly, making the game actually adaptive to individual learner performance. This is significant, as instead of tuning the challenge to the average performer you can tune the game dynamically to the individual performer.

There are a wide variety of ways to implement the underlying models. The underlying representation may be mathematical or it may be causal, but you'll need control logic to represent it so the computer can implement it, and that means programs or code. We may use numbers, rules, or both. And we can use a number of tools. We can use an Excel spreadsheet, modeling software such as Stella, or rule-based environments such as StageCast's Creator or AgentSheets. We can use general-purpose programming environments such as Java, specialized environments such as artificial intelligence (AI) (for example, Prolog, LISP), or graphics (for example, Flash) environments. In conjunction with students, I have built games in HyperCard and re-implemented one in HTML (HyperText Markup Language) with CGI (Common Gateway Interface) scripts in the background. Don't worry if you don't know some of these terms, by the way; the point here is to talk about design, not implementation. We will get pragmatic in Chapter Seven and touch on some implementation details, but the important thing for now is to figure out how to get the design right. There will be lots of different ways to implement the design. The critical, and difficult, thing is to get the design right.

Building Models

Regardless of how you implement it, however, you do need to know how to specify it. You will need to specify some initial values, how those values are

When you specify the underlying models, you include certain parameters that you preset to certain values at the beginning. Take it as a given that you will want to change the values of these parameters as you adjust the game play to get the right balance of difficulty, the right timing and frequency of occurrences, the right adjustment to variables, and so forth. For instance, you might determine that the adjustment to the score for a correct answer is to add one. It turns out that from an implementation standpoint, coders tend to write those values in every place they're needed. So, throughout the code, when there is a change to the value, they'll indicate the exact change. However, it makes it very hard to update the values once you start tuning, say if you then decide the right change is to increment by two. Good programmers will naturally use elegant design and instead assign these values to constants, and then refer to the constants instead of the values. They'll create a constant called something like *correct_increment*, which will initially be set to 1 (for example, *correct_increment = 1*) and then change the score everywhere by *score = score + correct_increment*. Once this is done, you can make changes easily to the constants (they're set in one place in the program, usually at the beginning, so all you have to do is find that one line and change *correct_increment = 1* to *correct_increment = 2*). Recommend to your implementation team that you will be tuning, and that they should be using modular design and constants.

affected by actions of the learner, any probabilities for random events, and which values or conditions constitute a successful (or unsuccessful) termination point for the game. We can, of course, make the design more complicated, specifying changes in probabilities depending on conditions, or adapting the difficulty based upon a learner's performance. Our goal should be to generate decision opportunities based upon some model of a situation (Figure 5-12).

Figure 5-12. Game Engine.

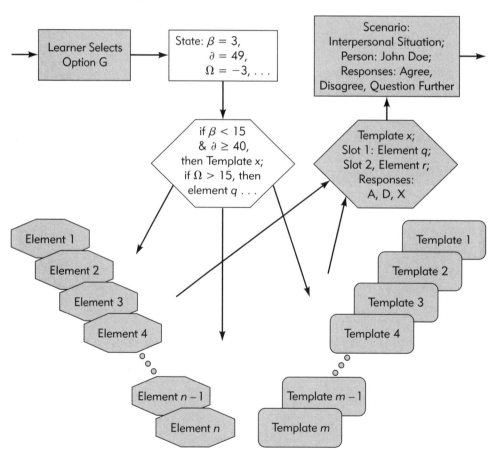

In this model, we see that we have a database of elements and some templates. Doing some underlying calculation (the formulas in the boxes are representative, not real), we choose a template for the next decision and populate that template with appropriate elements to create the learners' next decision.

For example, in a project management game (based on the initial linear scenario in Case Study 3), there was a basic template about evaluating the data for a particular project and then additional templates for stakeholder queries, budget overruns, schedule overruns, and so on. Thus, in addition to a recurrent decision about each project in the timeline (checking the data), other ones were thrown in probabilistically or as a result of some outcome of a previous decision. We populated these decision or situation templates with elements of project names, the character involved in this situation, the amounts, and so on. The characters and projects were pulled randomly from pools of each that were created to populate the game. The amounts were calculated from initial values generated for each project at the start of the game and then modified as the issue warranted by formulas and rules. The resulting experience is essentially infinite in combination, yet fairly simple sets of data and rules yield complex behavior and play. And *that* is the point of a game engine.

CASE STUDY 5

Drug Therapy Demo

My client this time was LearningMate, an e-learning solution provider to higher education. They were looking to augment their offerings in a substantially new way.

Context

LearningMate had a mainstay business in developing the Web sites that publishers provide to supplement textbooks. These Web sites contain things such as PowerPoint slide decks for the instructors, as well as question banks for exams. LearningMate had the foresight to be concerned that the publishers generally gave these materials away free and that this was not sustainable. The goal was a new product offering around which a viable business model could be built. We spent some time reviewing learning and what elements might augment learning to create a uniquely valuable offering. Many technology applications to support learning had already been developed, but what was not reliably present was an environment in which learners could practice their skills.

We wanted to develop learning scenarios to augment textbooks and provide compelling, effective, and repeatable practice for learners. This particular project was to develop a demonstration scenario around a relevant topic for LearningMate's client. In this case, a sample textbook was used, and the topic of drug use in medical practice was chosen. In particular, the topic was analgesics, and the specific drug of example was morphine.

Constraints

There had been previous efforts to develop practice environments for learners. In some cases, faculty would get grants to develop these projects, or a multi-talented faculty member would program one of their own volition. Publishers had attempted a number of examples, but they either were limited as branching scenarios or got quite expensive in developing the underlying model. We had to develop the technology and an associated process that could repeatedly, reliably, and scalably produce scenarios to accompany textbooks.

We had some freedom to draw on the talented graphic design, instructional design, and software skills of the production team in India. Our working concept was that we would not model an entire domain, for instance all of the chemical interactions of morphine with the human body, but instead templatize the decisions into a finite set of scenes, have them populated from databases with randomness to create variability, and have rules that linked the scenes together to create the learning experience.

Design Process

We started with a process that asks the subject matter expert (SME) to inform us about the learning objectives in the form of important decisions that learners would be able to make, contexts in which those decisions would occur, and information about the learners, both their motivations and their interests. We found that the particular decisions for this drug typically happen in the patient's hospital room. We also found out that this drug has particular implications for the elderly, and that the major complications are respiratory.

We worked up this information into a hospital setting where learners would be faced with patients with different demographics and characteristics. To do this we needed to come up with initial values and rules. For example, the values include starting variables for the learner's performance and various levels of the patient, including pain level, respiratory status, and anxiety. Randomly the pain level could vary from one to ten, and the patient might have asthma or not. Patients start out with a little anxiety, but mistakes can aggravate the anxiety. The choice of morphine will affect the respiratory system, and if there is initial asthma, it will get worse.

The path was to mimic the actual practice tasks of the learner, so the patient's medical chart was made available, as was the doctor's prescription. The learner then went to meet the patient (see Figure 5-13) and begin the actual scenario. The learner had the task to make a decision about the specific drug to be given and the dosage. The learner also had some choices about how to talk to the patient and what steps would accompany any choices and side effects. Information on the drugs was available, and the learner could also access the medical record and prescription. A separate character, a nursing supervisor, provides feedback about choices if things get too out of hand and also at the end. The actual behavior of the patient provides feedback, too.

In this sample screen, you see that the layout includes a graphic context image in the top (the image is masked to, er, protect the patient's privacy, yes, that's it). Below are the prompts for action and the choices. The graphic

CASE STUDY 5, Continued

Figure 5-13. Meet the Patient.

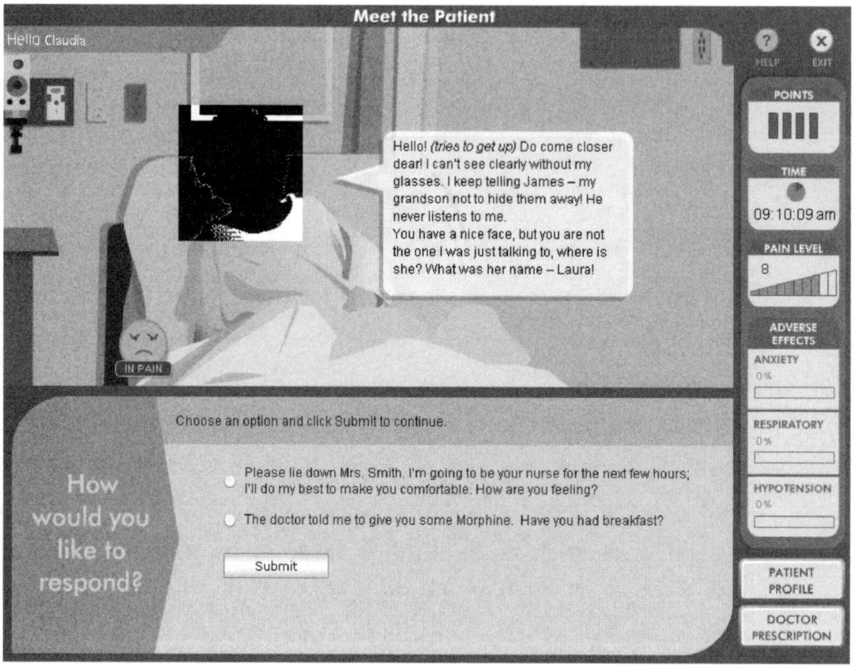

Source: LearningMate, Mumbai, India. Reproduced with permission.

updates with the result of the action (the patient might be happier or more concerned, you might have the head nurse intervene), while the story is played out in the lower half. On the right is a "control panel" that provides readouts and alternative opportunities, such as viewing the patient's medical history and doctor's prescription.

We made the underpinnings obvious in this case so that you actually had a window on the anxiety level and respiratory status of the patient, as well as her pain level. We did this as partly a marketing mechanism to demonstrate that the values changed randomly on different uses and after user actions. Of course, it could also be a teaching tool, with that support gradually being withdrawn.

I was partnered on this development by Debbie Zimmerman, who had prior content development experience and a computer science background. Not only was she diligent about working out the details, but also her technical background made it easy for her to think in terms of variables and rules. You don't need the technical background, but you absolutely need to be systematic and resolute, and I'm thankful that Debbie was brilliant at both.

For instance, the rules used included these:

- If ibuprofen 400 mg then Pain Level = Pain Level −1
- If morphine 4 gm administered then Pain Level = Pain Level −4, Respiratory = Respiratory + 20 percent (Respiratory), Hypotension = Hypotension + −20 percent (Hypotension)
- If pain > 5 then Anxiety = Anxiety + 2
- If Anxiety > 7 then go to Patient Panics

Outcomes

The first positive feedback came during the development of the demonstration. The subject matter expert (SME) had expressed skepticism over these types of products. After working through the first part of the process, however, she was excited about the possibilities!

We have shown this demonstration at a variety of venues. Although the experience is difficult to describe, actually seeing (and better yet playing with) the demo is a powerful communication tool for the experience and the learning power of this approach. A wide variety of groups have been excited about this demo in particular and these scenarios in general.

It is interesting that when we showed the demo to individuals experienced in nursing, they argued that the details were not quite right. This is partly because we only had the SME at the beginning, and tuning requires later interaction with the SME, and this was a demo. However, this is also partly because, as one individual informed us, the field of nursing is highly opinionated and that you'd be unlikely to get nursing experts to agree on much! Remember *that* the next time you go for treatment . . .

The ability to generate these scenarios for any learning objective, at a very effective price point, reliably and repeatedly is a major advantage Learning-Mate has developed.

Trade-offs

Don Norman has talked elegantly about design trade-offs (1990). My take on considering alternatives for design is that there are no right answers, only trade-offs. So, too, with levels. Game engines are an ideal, and while they can be done more simply than many expect, they also still require considerable effort. Many times, contingent scenarios are good enough, and we may often have to settle for linear scenarios or even mini-scenarios. These are still an improvement over traditional knowledge tests and at the mini-scenario and even linear scenario level require little more effort than writing simple multiple-choice questions.

Note also that the hard line between linear and contingent scenarios is somewhat arbitrary, and I have made scenarios that were linear in parts and branching in parts. The important thing is to be flexible to meet the constraints. You want a solution, not an abstractly correct and pragmatically unworkable solution. The goal is to get engaged learning!

6

A Design Process

I F WE WANT TO DEVELOP GAMES, or even one of the levels of scenarios, how do we go about it? Although it would be wonderful to think that having been given a framework anyone is now capable of designing games, my experience tells me otherwise. However, I also believe that there are systematic steps that can be used to guide design. Instructional design models are frameworks that provide support to ensure learning outcomes. Here I present an e-learning game design model that I similarly believe increases the likelihood of an engaging and effective learning experience.

I start with the basics of design and then talk about how you modify the design process to accommodate. The going is a little bit theoretical, and you can skip straight to the resulting model, but for those interested, the derivation offers some insight into the result and provides a firmer foundation from which to adapt to your own needs and circumstances.

Design Basics

The basic design process is to analyze the need, specify a solution, and implement the solution. This sort of one-pass model has been referred to as the waterfall model, where the output of one stage cascades into the next (Figure 6-1). However, such a model has been rejected under scrutiny, at least for systems that have human interfaces. That includes what we're doing, so we need to find an improved approach to design.

Figure 6-1. Waterfall Design Model.

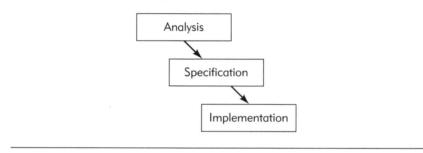

Realization of the complexity of most design processes has suggested some revisions. The first step is to evaluate the design to ensure that it meets the criteria that are determined in the analysis phase. Of course, if the system does not meet those criteria, a second (at least) pass through the steps may be required. The unpredictability of humans has led to iterative design processes that are an ongoing cycle of design, evaluation, and redesign (Figure 6-2).

This raises the question, When should you *stop* iterating? If we accept an interactive design cycle and want to avoid pursuing the four major stages in an endless cycle, we need to establish the parameters within these stages. This leads us to unpack the component stages.

Figure 6-2. Design Cycle.

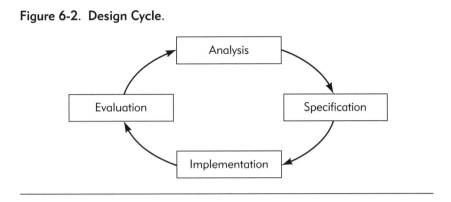

As a side note, there are lots of different models of the design process. Some of them are flow charts, others are cycles, some are even spirals, showing different ways of thinking about the design process. Some capture certain elements better, whereas others capture other elements better. The spiral model shows how we move from more preliminary specifications to more concrete implementations (see Figure 6-3).

Figure 6-3. Design Spiral.

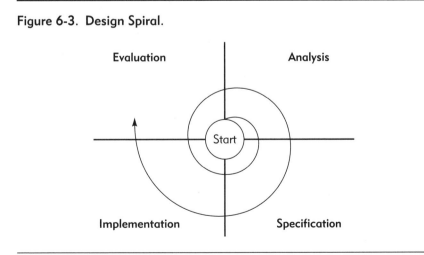

In the design process, teams are increasingly used to develop the outcome. Sometimes the same teams will carry a project from beginning to end, and at other times there are handoffs from marketing to engineering to usability to market. We are more often seeing diverse teams (the call for concurrent engineering is an indication of this) that bring together different strengths to provide all the necessary input.

Design Stages

From here, we need to look at the component stages of design: analysis, specification, implementation, and evaluation.

Analysis

Analysis means that we try to understand the problem, identify all relevant parameters, collect relevant data, conduct observations, and generally ensure we have considered all the issues that might affect the success of our design. We also need to digest these data to ensure that we understand the criteria for an effective and efficient solution—including, by the way, any and all constraints on finances and calendar. Our design must meet criteria that achieve a goal under pragmatic constraints of time and resources. Once we iterate, analysis is the part of the process where we take our initial data from evaluation and determine what they tell us.

There are a wide variety of methods used to gather the appropriate information. We may be given some time constraints ("The product releases in four weeks, we need the training by then") or budget constraints ("We need a solution, but we only have $30K available in the budget"). The nature of the problem should dictate some of the elements of the desired solution. Of course, we also have a learning goal, or an identified performance gap (since this process designs a learning solution, it assumes a learning need).

We may also need to gather some additional data. Who's the solution for? How are things currently done? We may need to observe people in action (ethnographic methods such as contextual inquiry) or get some of the target audience involved in the solution (participatory design). The richer the data collected, the better off we are in our design process. Of course, there are usually limits to how long we can spend doing research before we need to demonstrate progress.

We also must analyze these data to determine what our design goals must be. The output of the analysis process should be a set of criteria for our solution. Some of the most important criteria are the performance measures by which we know we've succeeded. Many times in design the iterative cycle ends when time or money run out. However, the proper criteria for ending iteration are when the initial criteria are met. In this phase we need to set the criteria for the solution, including the measurable objectives that indicate an acceptable level of performance. These objectives can then be tested against the metrics to determine whether we have achieved the goals of the design process.

In developing products, several types of measures have been important. Typically, the top categories are

- Ease of use (measured as time to perform tasks or tasks per time)

- Ease of learning (time taken to get to a specific level of performance)

- Retention over time (time taken to get to a new level of performance, or percentage of tasks able to be performed after a particular time, after achieving a prior level of performance)

- Errors (below a certain number over a set number of tasks or time)

- User experience (a subjective measure comparing the experience to other relevant experiences)

For our purposes, we'll be primarily focused on ease of learning and user experience. We should choose our criteria now, in the analysis phase. Our criteria for learning will be somewhat different, but we should establish some metrics that we can measure in the evaluation phase to determine that we're done.

The output of the analysis phase is a set of criteria that a solution must meet.

Specification

Specification is the creative part of the design cycle, and what people typically think of when they think of design. Here is where we attempt to find a workable solution to the criteria arising from the analysis phase.

In this phase, we need to diverge and generate a wide variety of alternatives that cover the potential solution space. Then we need to evaluate representative solutions and converge on a design solution. This process, too, can be iterative. We may generate a set of alternatives, evaluate them, and then select a subset to refine further. An interface design firm I knew used to have parallel teams design two independent solutions before meeting to design which, or which elements, of the solutions would be carried forward.

There are a number of ways to think about the design process relative to this discussion. One is to think of design as a problem-solving process to find a solution to the design problem that the criteria established in the analysis phase. This suggests some of the known results from problem-solving, such as time to incubate, re-representing the problem, and so forth. It also suggests some design traps, such as functional fixedness, whereby we tend to see tools in a particular way and miss new applications, and set effects, in which previous solutions tend to bias us to those methods. Another way is to think about design as a search through a space of possible solutions. This perspective helps us think about ways to help ensure a thorough search.

One of the most common techniques to generate potential designs is called brainstorming. The general idea is to generate as many ideas as possible. We also know several things about how to optimize brainstorming. For instance, you should review the goals beforehand. It's also better to brainstorm in a group rather than try to do it alone. However, you should do it alone first, then share the results in a group. We know that we should not evaluate any of the generated ideas until we've stopped generating. Introducing some randomness into the brainstorming process helps us escape from some simple mental traps. A proposed brainstorming process that integrates these components is listed in Exhibit 6-1.

Exhibit 6-1. Brainstorming Process.

Include creative people on your team and look for diversity, too

Circulate your criteria for a solution

Have your team brainstorm individually

Allow time for incubation

Set aside several hours of time as a group to work undisturbed

Get together and review criteria

Do a warm-up or loosen-up exercise

(Note: throughout this idea generation, no evaluation of the ideas)

(Collect all the generated ideas, ideally in a representation format all can view)

Share the individual thoughts

Look for any ideas that arise from the individual contributions

Look for any connections between ideas that create alternatives

Deliberately try to generate wild ideas

Use juxtaposition of random ideas to suggest alternatives (e.g., What does 'red tennis shoe' suggest about the idea?)

When all possible ideas are generated, then move into evaluation

One of the interesting results of work on design is that adding constraints to the design process can be helpful. If the solution space is too big, adding constraints helps limit the space we have to search, and searching is time-consuming. Too many stipulations, however, may constrain the search space into the empty set. Then, of course, we have to loosen some constraints.

The old project management triangle of scope, resources, and schedule is pertinent. If you can't meet all three elements of the triangle, you're going to have to loosen up one of them. We can try to loosen up resources or let the schedule slip, but sometimes we'll have to rein in the scope of the solution.

The design process often yields questions that need to be answered before the design can be finalized. The analysis phase cannot anticipate questions at every level, and some data will be needed. For instance, choosing how to provide menus: should they be pop-up or top-down? The ideal answer is always empirical, since situations vary so much. However, time and resource constraints on the process will often preclude complete (sometimes even most or all) empirical testing. Standards, guidelines, and heuristics (in that order) should be used to answer questions when possible (an early HCI [human-computer interaction] text suggested stealing any design solutions your lawyers would let you), but occasionally you will come up with questions that only empirical testing can answer (your intuition should not be used, on principle). Hence we have a need for iterative testing.

In fact, the purpose of every cycle through implementation and evaluation should be answering a set of design questions. Initially they will be questions such as, "Should we use this game model or that?" Later on they'll get to the level of, "Should this be placed here or there?" Finally, they should get to the level of, "Have we met our goals or not?" The output of the specification process is a proposal for a design implementation and a set of questions to be answered by the implementation.

Implementation

The implementation phase starts building a solution. This implementation needs a level of sophistication commensurate with the stage of the design. More specifically, you should implement in the lowest-cost approach that will

I'm an advocate of revolutionary prototyping, which at its strongest stance says you explicitly throw away all your prototypes. This rule can be violated *if* you have a powerful and easy development environment (rare). The pragmatic approach is to start technical development sometime before the final version but resist the temptation as much as possible and stick with the lowest technology as long as you can.

allow you to evaluate that level of design. *Low-fidelity* implementations start with imagination and move on through paper to gradually increasing technology. They're low in terms of their relationship to the final product, and eventually we'll want to move to *high-fidelity.* However, we should aim for the lowest level of technology possible that answers the question. It's a characteristic of technology implementation that the more you invest in a particular level of development, the less likely you are to change it, even if it turns out to be wrong. Thus, we want to maximize data and minimize investment as long as possible. If we've been going down the wrong path, it would be nice to know before a lot of programming has occurred.

As this book is about design, not production, I'll stop here except to re-iterate the point about using the lowest technology possible. When we get to pragmatics, I'll suggest some low-tech prototyping environments and how to use them. As mentioned earlier, implementation isn't usually the barrier. Coming up with the right design is the difficult task.

Evaluation

Once you have an implementation and questions to answer, you need to find a way to use the implementation to answer the questions; you need an evaluation process. This process comes into experimental design: How do you design a trial use of the prototype to get valid data that answer your question? It involves the right setting, the right controls, the right measures, and the right subjects. And although practical evaluation is somewhat different from scientific experiment design, you do want an approach that gives you confidence in your answers.

For science you want statistical significance. In practice, you want what I call "business" significance. Statistical significance is great, but if you don't have that option (you usually won't), you will at least want data you can use to convince an executive or other decision maker.

In many ways, the field of human-computer interaction (also known as usability) has led learning design. Its earlier work on cost justification has been a model for our work, and it has developed some great usability approaches. Techniques such as paper prototyping have been shown to be useful, for instance. I recommend checking out the field, as well as cultivating a mutually beneficial relationship with those folks. Eventually, I believe our goals will mesh when we realize *doing* is at the core of what both groups are about.

You need appropriate setups to conduct the data collection, appropriate measures, and an appropriate population of subjects. Ideally, you test the implementation with a representative sample of the end users. Practically, you take whomever you can get appropriate for the level of evaluation.

All of the constraints vary depending on where you are in the design cycle. Early on, you can use quick mock-ups and opinions or polls. Your prototypes will be simpler; your measures, more ad hoc; your population, more local and expedient. As you get to greater levels of development, you'll want more precise measures and greater approximations to your end users, eventually getting some real end users representative of the audience.

Our measures should correlate to the answers we need. We may need quantitative data ("Which of these two approaches is faster to accomplish the task?" "Which of these two metaphors leads to fewer errors?") or qualitative information ("Which of these two designs is more appealing?" "Does this line of humor work?"). We'll need ways to answer the questions that are appropriate to the type of question.

Repeat

We continue cycling through the stages until we achieve our predetermined performance. We could relabel our stages as re-analysis, re-specification, re-implementation, and re-evaluation (see Figure 6-4).

Figure 6-4. Iterative Design.

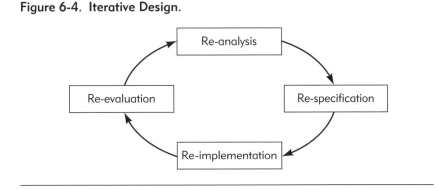

This is all a bit abstract at this point, but I want to establish a framework we can adjust for our needs.

Instructional Design

We start by reviewing a generalized instructional design process briefly. This is not the appropriate place to detail such processes (I refer the reader to many great texts on instructional design) (see Chapter Two), so I present a very abbreviated discussion that highlights the main points and emphasizes the modifications necessary to achieve the enhanced instructional design of the convergent model I developed in Chapter Two.

Instructional design, as a field, has worked hard to demonstrate that the approach is scientific and has come up with processes that should systematically lead to the required learning specification. The instructional design field has developed a prototypical approach to design called ADDIE: analysis, design, development, implementation, and evaluation. The development phase creates the materials, the implementation deploys them, and evaluation determines their effectiveness. It's a much more linear model than I believe in (and to be fair, I'm pretty sure they agree; eminent scholars such as Tom Reeves advocate a more iterative approach, such as design research). My approach is a smaller-scale approach, but I combine ADDIE's development and implementation into implementation.

Analysis

In this phase, the performance gap is analyzed, and the criteria for the learning improvement should be decided. As stated earlier, we're assuming that the performance gap is known, and now we're adding a stipulation that the knowledge level should be adjusted to develop a skill that will address the problem. In instructional design we frame things in behavioral objectives, as we saw in Chapter Two, where we specify

- Performance
- Conditions
- Criterion

Our inputs to the specification process are the behavioral objectives we need to achieve.

Specification

In this phase, we review the type of learning objective and the criteria for performance to determine the type of learning approach to take. Typically, you can look this up in a matrix such as David Merrill's component display theory, which maps type of knowledge and level of performance onto specific instructional interventions (Merrill, 1983).

Implementation

With the specification determined, we can create the actual materials. Whether print, electronic, or otherwise, we have models and tools that let us generate our learner experience.

Evaluation

Theoretically, our only evaluation is whether we have achieved our goal or not. With the systematic approach, this should serve merely as a validation.

Note that usability evaluation has to precede learning evaluation. If not, problems that appear might be attributable to the interface or the learning design. Ensure that the learners can execute the interface activities given appropriate goals before evaluating the learning outcomes.

Summary

Although this process is designed systematically, we know that much instructionally designed material is uninteresting, if not ineffective. This may be attributable to bad implementation of the design, but the cognitive research cited in Chapter Two suggests that this approach is limited. Practitioners like Michael Allen (2002) are moving in the direction of understanding and using affect.

The teams of instructional design usually are partnerships between subject matter experts (SMEs) and instructional designers. At times, other expertise will be brought to bear under the direction of the instructional designer, including media production (graphic design, animation, audio, and video) and technology expertise (software engineering, Web developers).

Engagement Perspective

The game industry's approach to design is pretty much in tune with the general process introduced above. The differences between educational and entertainment projects lead to some differences in approaches.

One of the advantages (or burdens) the game industry has is having bigger projects. The budgets are bigger, and the timelines are bigger. The game industry has surpassed Hollywood in revenue recently, and while the scale is smaller ($5–6 million is a typical game budget, versus an order of magnitude more at Hollywood, perhaps $50–60 million), the model's the same. Many games are made for every one that is a hit, and the hits support the rest of the games. Games can be in development for close to two years, sometimes longer. Movies usually take a year or less to produce once the funding is accomplished.

There are some similarities in the two design processes, too. In both cases, a document serves as an organizing element—a script in Hollywood and a

Note that there are significant differences in the design processes as well, and Hollywood writers can't automatically transition to writing games, just as game designers may not succeed as scriptwriters. David Freeman, in his book *Creating Emotion in Games*, points out the flaws on both sides (Freeman, 2004). One point I've heard made is that you need to distinguish between the background theme and the foreground action. You can't write a story for a game; while you establish a background story, the foreground activity is an interactive choice of options, all of which should have interesting arcs of their own.

design document in the gaming industry. The design document typically is the product of a single writer, at least initially, but it usually evolves more toward an agreed-upon concept than an independent vision. There is variability, of course. This document captures the essential vision and ideally is updated as the concept changes due to pressures that arise during development. The various components, such as graphics and AI, may end up being documented by different people from those areas.

With the long gestation times, many changes may occur in the context in which a game is being made. For example, one of the characteristics of the game industry is continual technological change and associated competition. It's not unknown for a competitor's release to create pressure for a new feature even late in the development process. Sponsors in the funding organization may change, as well, along with agendas. Also, certain ideas may test less excitingly (or more) than anticipated, and so require adaptation.

These constraints make the game design process a mix between ideal and pragmatic. There is less science about it than with instructional design, or at least less public reflection on how it's done. However, Earnest Adams (Rollings & Adams, 2003) and Chris Crawford (1990, 2003) are some of the most articulate writers of books on game design; they're worth your review. Only a rough sketch here will be given of the differences.

Analysis

The design process typically involves some game concept arising out of market research or, less frequently, from an individual vision. It usually has to be sold to a company to fund development, after which the team assembles to produce it. Unlike Hollywood, where the director has the artistic vision (leading to some interesting tensions with the producers at times) and a script, in game design there is more collaboration.

The criteria for games are more fluid. Instead of saying we have to address this particular market segment or learning need, it's more typical to determine that the right "hit" will be along the lines of a particular genre, using a particular technology. Sometimes a particular game is needed; for example, the next version of a sports game, or a game to accompany a licensed property (such as a movie or book title).

Specification

In this stage, a concept is developed and embodied in a design document that is taken to funding bodies (unless it is funded as long as it meets a license requirement). It's considered done when someone's funded the development. Everyone understands (or should) that the result may not be exactly what was intended, as development and circumstances may alter the plan.

Implementation

The implementation is typically done in higher technology environments early, as in general the technological underpinnings are part of the development. The game industry tends not to use established environments, but is continually trying to get a competitive advantage by creating a new level of capability out of the same hardware. Thus, the technology environment is often being developed simultaneously with the game concept. Ideally, these are done in synchrony.

Evaluation

Because commercial success is measured by player experience and lack of bugs, testing is a big part of the process. Quality control is very important; consequently "game tester" is an occupation, albeit a low-paid one. In addition to weeding out games, tuning the game play characteristics is key. Will Wright, designer of "SimCity" and "The Sims," once told me that programming is one-tenth of the work (and programming is huge) but tuning is nine-tenths of the work. Tuning requires regular testing, refinement, and more testing.

Summary

The scale of game projects is large, as are the teams. One of the big factors is the technology environment, which we can largely ignore here. Although we will have to get our designs produced, typically we will use existing technology. Thus, we can focus on the learning and engagement design.

Engaged Design: Creating Meaningful Practice

Integrating these two approaches, design for learning and design for engagement, requires using the framework introduced in Chapter Four to help align the processes. We will want to take the stages of the design process and determine what steps at each stage will lead to the desired outcome. We also have to decide which side leads (learning or engagement) and which side follows for various components of the design process. Most of our discussion will focus on the specification, but we will talk a bit about how adding engagement to learning affects the other stages as well.

The basic lesson is that getting learners to make decisions is key. We want the learning to require that learners apply the knowledge to make a decision, not just test their knowledge. And they learn by the consequences of their decision, right or wrong. For example, we do not want learners to be able to recite the principles of "solution selling" (moving from pushing product to identifying and solving the customer's problem), but instead to make choices that reflect an *understanding* of solution selling. There are some potentially subtle but substantial differences between the two, as we see in the following table (Table 6-1).

Table 6-1. Knowledge Test Versus Knowledge Application.

Knowledge Test	Knowledge Application
Asks for concept	Asks for action
Distractors are other concepts	Distractors are common misconceptions
States the question	Story sets up decision
Wrong or right	Feedback in context of story

A critical component of this approach at all levels is that we place the learning in context. We want to have the decision to mimic as best as possible the application of the knowledge, as it will occur after the learning experience. The decision should ideally engage the learner's interest and be an application of the knowledge that will transfer effectively to other opportunities to apply the knowledge.

Recognize that the story has to set up the key activity on the part of the learner making decisions. The theme has to provide, directly or indirectly, the goals for the scenario, a context in which the decisions make sense and tie together, and roles for the protagonist (the player's character) and other characters who can be antagonists to the protagonist, as well as other characters who may be examples or sources of feedback.

Which is not to say, of course, that it has to be absolutely true to the actual application context. In many cases we may make up stories that are exaggerated or outright fantastic. So if the knowledge is a component to the ultimate understanding that will be applied, we may need to provide a reason for this component knowledge that does not exist in the setting.

For example, in partnership with a client we were developing understanding of ultrasound technology and the component parts of frequency and transducer technology (piezoelectric crystals are substances that vibrate when electricity is applied). We needed a situation in which one would apply this component knowledge, but learners were not yet ready for the advanced inferences that were the ultimate expression of the concepts. So we created an artificial situation in which there was a robot-run ultrasound instrument construction and repair facility where humans served to oversee the robotic decisions. Robots can be as stupid or as smart as you need them, so they could require some fairly basic decisions. This setting might not appeal to any audience but technologists, but we felt it would work for people who enjoy the application of science to the design of useful instruments.

Another way to think about it, as Henry Jenkins from MIT's Games to Teach project suggested in a conference presentation, is that you choose the right role for the player to take. That is, a role that the player would want to assume in which he or she would be making the appropriate types of decisions. That is also a role where the game can have ways to believably simplify the world (not violating the willingness to suspend disbelief).

We also need the learner to viscerally understand why this knowledge is important. One of the things we can do is ramp up the drama to really exaggerate the importance of the material. For instance, instead of conducting epidemiology for a normal disease, we could set the task in the situation of a bioterrorism attack. We can also tie it to situations that the audience understands is important because of the audience's characteristics.

One of the things to emphasize is that feedback from learners' decisions should also come in the form of the story. The reflection may be external, but the feedback should be set in the thematic or model world. Even in a mini-scenario, instead of providing the feedback externally (for example, "You chose to approach the vice president, and this is wrong because the vice president has already delegated decision making and budgetary authority to the line manager.") you write your feedback as a consequence of the story ("Chris, the line manager, gets back to you and asks, 'Why did you go to the VP? I've already got the approval. You ended up getting me in trouble since the VP's time was wasted.'").

Another important point is choosing the distractors for your decisions. In many cases, multiple-choice questions are written with other, wrong concepts as easy alternatives. However, pedagogically we'd like to not make easy discriminations but instead catch the problems learners typically make (which sometimes is, and sometimes is not, choosing the wrong concept). The right alternative choices, particularly to get the right level of challenge for learners, are the common misconceptions that learners have. Put another way, the issue is to deal with those problems the instructor or the mentors of the audience continue to observe despite the teaching. If they're not yet known, get the best guess of the SME as to where they'll go wrong.

One of the hardest things initially is getting in the habit of changing knowledge-level objectives into contextualized decisions. The trick is to ask yourself, or the SME: Where and how would (or could) the learner actually use this knowledge? Let's work through several examples.

Say the sales department brings you a set of new product specifications that they want you to get their sales folks to learn, and they dump a bunch of presentations and fact sheets on you. They want the sales force to quickly get up to speed on the data. The usual approach is to present the sales force with a lot of content about the new specifications. However, if we apply the rubric of thinking about how the learners might use the specifications, we get into more interesting opportunities. For instance, imagine that product A now supports the range of 50 to 75 psi (pounds per square inch), whereas product B covers the range of 30 to 60 psi. Let's say a company has a particular need, which translates into a quantitative requirement such as 55 psi. Which product should the salesperson recommend? Then, what if the psi requirement is 45? Putting the salesperson into the role of consulting with a client and being presented with the need and having to choose whether to push product A or B makes the salesperson think through the implications of the specifications and motivates him or her to pay attention to the new numbers.

Or say there is a new series of ethical behavior codes that have been enforced in your industry. The legal group wants the employees to demonstrate knowledge of the codes to avoid investigation or litigation. They give you the details about acceptable and nonacceptable behavior as a series of codes. Instead of presenting the codes and doing a knowledge test, think about how they should apply the knowledge. Consider putting employees in circumstances that are opportunities to exercise knowledge about how to behave, and ask them what actions they'd take, for instance, if offered tickets to a game by a salesperson. Should they accept the offer, believing that it is harmless? Should they report it to their boss? Should they just say "no thanks"?

If it's important and the task is difficult (in other words, the challenge is too much), you may start with coarser distinctions that are easier to discriminate and gradually make them finer. We can, conversely, make the distinctions more difficult by confounding the choice with some ambiguity or confounding constraints.

Now, how do we go about developing this into a systematic and repeatable process?

Engaged Design: The Process

A design process that synergistically melds engagement and learning must first gather the information needed to understand the audience, collect the objectives at a high enough level, and establish appropriate criteria to determine success. Then the process must support exploring alternative solutions and add the extra details that enhance the experience. The implementation must allow for suitable fidelity for testing at the appropriate stage, and finally the evaluation methods must correlate to the joint goals. At a coarse cut, the stages are as shown in Exhibit 6-2 (more detail is found in Exhibit 6-4).

Exhibit 6-2. Learning Game Design Stages and Steps.

Analysis
    Determine target performance
    Determine learner characteristics
    Determine learner interests
    Establish metrics
Specification
    Situate the task in a model world
    Elaborate the details
    Incorporate underlying pedagogical support

Exhibit 6-2. Learning Game Design Stages and Steps, *Continued*.

Map learning to interface
(Build the model)

Implementation
    Prototype

Evaluation
    Test for usability
    Test for educational effectiveness
    Test for engagement

Thus, the main determinations for the analysis phase are the target performance, learner characteristics, and learner interests. The latter are the unique contribution, although we have focused on decisions (and misconceptions), and we'll want to know more about learner motivations and characteristics as well. Then, in specification, we need to consider the optimal setting in which to make the learners make these decisions and also hit all the engagement points. We'll want to make sure we provide learners with the full pedagogical support (though not all has to come from the experience environment), and we'll want to make sure that the actions of the learners map appropriately to the learning objectives. We must prototype our solution to support our evaluation. Finally, we evaluate not just the learning but also the experience.

Analysis

To begin, we assume that we have identified a learning objective or knowledge need, and our first task is to ensure that it has been mapped to a skill. We need to ensure that we have an objective we can use. We also want to know our audience. This time it's not just their knowledge we want to assess but also their motivations and interests.

Scientists distinguish between three sorts of characteristics of an individual: their *cognitive*, *conative*, and *affective* components. Cognitive components are what individuals know and know how to do, as well as their capabilities. Conative components address an individual's innate motivations. Affective components tend to be who people are, their personality types and preferences. Addressing a richer suite of these is an important component in personalizing the learning experience (discussed in Chapter Eight).

We want to frame our learning goal as a behavioral objective but focused on using the knowledge or skill to *do* something. We may need to inquire to ensure that the decisions are indeed the right ones, but we assume that the problem has already been identified. If it's a whole process, we need to know the different decisions made during the process, the criteria that would make you choose one over the other, and what the consequences are for the wrong decision. We also absolutely critically need to know what are the wrong responses we typically see from the learners, and why.

It's been shown that although learners can make mistakes because they weren't paying attention, a more important reason they make mistakes is because they have a perfectly logical, sensible reason for why they did things that just happens to be wrong. Learners will create stories or mental models about how things work, but they can get them wrong. Once created, however, these models are hard to extinguish. Getting things wrong in the learning environment is one point at which you have an opportunity to address their misconceptions. So it's important to find out what the misconceptions are, and why, so you can provide the appropriate (story-based) feedback.

Sometimes, the learning environment is only part of a blended solution, and there will be live or face-to-face training to get into the nuances. Recognize what role the solution plays, and specify accordingly.

We may have to assist in getting the objective up to a meaningful level. The key is to ask what a learner would *do* with that knowledge. When the sales team says that they need to know the parameters of the new product, we need to ask what they will do with that knowledge. When teachers say their students have to know this fact, ask what they will do with that knowledge. Find the use context as key to designing the learning experience.

We also want to see what other objectives may make sense to add into the environment. Some complexity adds to the challenge of the game, but the complexity of developing the implementation goes up essentially geometrically with each additional objective. So, too, does the cost. Note that it is easy to try to incorporate too many objectives. The situation gets particularly heinous at tuning time, where you have many more factors to try to have work in synchrony. More important, extra objectives may obscure your main point. Rigorously prune objectives to those that have a clear benefit, unless you have more money and time than you know what to do with (and if that's the case, please call me, as I can help).

That said, if the play is too simple, having extra objectives can be a vehicle for adding challenge. Consequently, collect more secondary objectives than you need, but recognize which ones are critical. Then incorporate extra objectives as you need to, but don't expect to be able to use any or all of them. For instance, in the "Quest" game (Case Study 1, Chapter Four), in addition to maintaining food and sleep levels and acquiring money, there was the opportunity to have sex and drugs, but not much else. Similarly, in the "Project Management for Non-Project Managers" game, we added dealing with difficult people, but not, for instance, having them actually calculate times or costs. The scope of your solution will determine how much latitude you have for layering on additional objectives, but it's very easy to load on too many, and I recommend erring on the side of caution until you determine you can handle what you need and discover you need complexity before you go searching for it. Complexity will generally find you.

Exhibit 6-3 is a questionnaire I've used to try to help get the types of answers needed to move into the specification phase.

Exhibit 6-3. Game Design Analysis Questionnaire.

What makes these people get up in the morning? Just who are these learners? For example, personality types: detail, conceptual, social, retiring, and so forth.

What role does this content play in the performance on the job?

What would be the activity that would most assist learners in passing any relevant assessment or certification?

What would be the activity that would most help learners link this content to tasks as seen in practice?

What is a set of situations that would have the learners thoroughly exercise the skills?

What is the primary objective this content is supposed to meet? Are there any secondary ones?

Within each situation, what are the different decisions learners would need to make? For each, what is the context for the decision? What is the setup that will make the decision clear and compelling? What is the right answer? What is the appropriate feedback?

What reliable wrong responses to those decisions do learners make? Why? In what contexts? For each wrong response, what is the feedback to remediate that misconception?

Once we understand the learners, decisions, contexts, and misconceptions, we're ready to start creating a setting in which to exercise these skills.

Specification

With decisions and contexts in hand, it's now time to find a story line, setting, theme, and model world in which to set these decisions. We need to consider as wide a variety of appropriate situations as we can (within realistic bounds) for the reasons mentioned earlier about the traps we can fall into as designers.

Design the Experience. The key issue is to think about creating a situation that places the learner in a compelling experience, one that has the features we identified in Chapter Four. You want to think of the flow of the learner's experience throughout the game. What is a situation in which a character would make decisions like the ones we need, in a setting that makes the decisions meaningful and of interest to the learner?

Earnest Adams (Adams, 2004) suggests that there are three major elements in defining game play: a *perspective* or view (typically either first person or an omniscient view from above or the side); an *interaction model* or ways in which the player acts on the world; and finally the *game play* itself, the series of "interesting decisions," as he quotes Sid Meier. These elements characterize the overall experience.

Depending on the directness of transfer (to how many different types of situations we want it to apply in), we may make the theme more concrete or more fanciful. That is to say, if it is a specific business skill (talking customers through our application), we might have to make the story fairly concrete. If it is a more generic skill, such as negotiation, we have leeway to make it more fantastic. Note that the more general the skill is (the further we would want it to transfer in terms of appropriate other situations), the more we need situations that differ as much as possible in all possible dimensions that still make an appropriate application. As mentioned before in Chapter Two, that will facilitate abstraction of the underlying concept and consequently transfer. An ideal approach might be to make several very different games. A more practical approach may be to choose or design a setting in which such variance makes sense.

We also need to consider the genre, as discussed in Chapter Three. Is it a mystery, dramatic encounter, or sports theme? To teach auto repair, I proposed a future freeway race (with heavily armed mini-vans). To teach computer auditing, the authors created a detective game.

Note that we'll want a setting that mines the characteristics of the audience and matches their motivations and interests. For an audience of engineers, I set a project management game in space, since the learning goal was indirect and the story line was generally appealing (see Case Study 3 in Chapter Five). For an audience of engineers assisting sales, the setting was in business, as a primary theme was for them to learn to understand executive concerns.

There's little more to be said here than to use the creativity processes we know about and look to a wide range of dramatic arts for inspiration. Use the process shown in Exhibit 6.1. This is the fun stuff, of course. Years ago, when I was working my first job out of college designing educational computer games, the CEO, Jim Schuyler, gave us each a roll of quarters and sent us to the local video game arcade for inspiration. You now have justification to play games, watch movies, read novels, and keep up with popular culture: it's fodder for the design process!

As an outcome, you should have at least one and ideally several good ideas. Flesh them out to a description of the user experience at a top level. Create a rough story board of every decision point and provide sample choices. The story board, at some point in the iterations, can begin to capture at least wire-frame versions of the interface. One approach is to have separate teams work on competitive ideas.

Note that documenting your design is critical for several interlocking reasons. For one, it makes you get concrete about thoughts that you think you understand. It also helps team members share their understanding, so you avoid the problem of the blind men and the elephant (they all agree it's an elephant, but the one holding the tail thinks it's like a rope, the one touching the leg thinks it's like a tree, the one at the trunk thinks it's like a snake, and so on). Much discussion often follows documenting a design that everyone thought they understood. Another reason comes from maintaining focus as the team works along. Research into why products went awry or were late

Wire frames are graphics that block out the major components of the screen without specifying the details within. So space might be left for a navigation bar and a graphic, along with an area for dialogue and for choices, without fleshing out the details within. Figure 5.6 is the result of adding graphic trappings to a wire frame without really identifying what content would actually go into it.

revealed that teams on extended designs would begin to revisit decisions made earlier as they reemerged, or as the team composition changed. A new field, design rationale, arose that argued for keeping records of the design as it developed (tools such as issue-based information systems [IBIS] were even used to track them).

Sweat the Details. There are a number of steps that must be taken to develop the details. Simultaneously you must hew to the story line, create believable characters, find ways to ensure that the challenge and interest are appropriate, and include some randomness. You also have to ensure that supporting materials are thematically coherent, as well as integral—and, of course, identify and build in those misconceptions and consequences thereof.

You'll want to ensure that you have the story line as compelling as necessary to appeal to the audience. One of the easy tricks is to make the rationale for the decision more immediate: if you're talking about business, your company is about to go under; in medicine there is an outbreak or a serious accident; in government there is corruption to be sniffed out or previous mistakes to fix. You may not always want to ramp it up as much as possible, but instead keep it toned down for a particular audience.

You may also want to play with adjusting the challenge. In literature, the tension increases then releases while following a gradual overall increase (see Figure 3-1). Our challenge should get harder to match the learner's challenge, and the periods of feedback may serve as surcease, but think through the overall learner experience as one of the checks on the design.

Even if you aren't having a full underlying model, consider having the outcomes of some decisions slightly eccentric or even silly (as long as the message still is communicated). Novelty helps maintain interest, and humor can be used (sparingly and carefully). For instance, if players wrongly choose to go straight to the vice president before checking with their manager, you can have them catch the vice president doing something untoward (like watching sports, what were *you* thinking?) and have them sent back to the appropriate person in the reporting chain with an embarrassed and angry response. Or have a clip of a real vice president of the company talking to the learners.

You will want to consider using media to help establish the theme. Consider photos, graphics, audio clips, video clips, or animation, as your budget will support. These should not be gratuitous: you want to help communicate the context, not overload the learner's cognitive capacity, so you'll want to ensure that all the components of the solution match the setting and theme. Even if you use text and static stock photographs to illustrate a page, ensure that the font, layout, and photographs are appropriate to the setting. You don't want bright smiling people if it's a dire situation. You don't want gothic fonts on a modern story. Appropriate sound effects can assist in communicating but can distract if not supportive of the story line. Note that the extra elements should not be intruding at times when the learner is making decisions or you'll overload their cognitive capacity, unless there is a reason to raise the challenge level or the final performance environment similarly has these intrusions (that is, the performance context matches the practice context, in which case you may need to develop the skills before adding these additional complications or in smaller chunks).

You also want to develop the ancillary elements of the story: any score-keeping or other activities. These need to be set in a way that is coherent with the story. If they're slapped on without grounding in the context of the story, they can be disruptive. It is possible to make such elements fit or be contrary to the theme, and yet extrinsic elements detract.

This is best illustrated with an example. A game was set up that had the players competing on knowledge, and they had to progress along a fixed but abstract path. In keeping with the elements of novelty, the player could be randomly moved forward or backward a step or two from time to time. In the game was a character who had a vested interest in the player completing the game. However, the story line, when I reviewed the design, had that character actively being responsible for the random movements forward or back. This seemed contrary to the character's overall motivation! This character was also involved in activities that could alter the fabric of the universe. I suggested that side effects from those activities could be used to randomly move the players back or forward, which was still in coherence with the game story but more in coherence with the character's motivations. The point being, the more you can cause the events in the game to be a consequence of the player actions or the context (and not capriciously in conflict with story elements), the more coherent and consequently acceptable your product will be.

Many times, characters besides the *avatar,* the player's character, will be part of the game. The general guideline is to develop the characters a bit further than you actually need. Particularly for any character that plays a significant role in the game, it helps to think about where they came from and what's happened to them along the way to understand who they are now. They also should not be completely one way or another; they are more interesting if they have a slight aberrant tendency. Give them appropriate names, which can mean even funny or odd ones. One of the elements of literature is that characters develop and change over time. Particularly for the protagonist in a story, the change is supposed to be fundamental. In the course of a game that may be a bit much, but learners are changing their behavior through learning, so find ways to signify that. You can have the avatar get promoted or rewarded for astute performance in the game and similarly punished for poor performance.

In developing the story line, you'll also have to embed the misconceptions in the decisions. The misconceptions should have been identified in the analysis phase and already be allocated to each decision. You'll probably have to specify what the various consequences of the actions are in terms of their effect on the story line. These consequences should lead to other decisions or the various final outcomes (for example, success or failure). If you don't have enough to make a plausible list of alternatives, you may need some others. Consider, for the sake of reality, having an action not taken earlier be still relevant (or even more relevant) later on. For instance, you're expecting a package, and from the options you first decide to check the mailroom. When you still can't find it, you decide to check the delivery status on the shipper's Web site (an option you had the first time).

Essentially, when you finish, you should have a template or story board (see below) that, in a richly elaborated story line, lists the sequence of decisions and consequences thereof. You may not include all the elaborations, but having done the work you're more likely to not make errors in the overall implementation.

Incorporate Pedagogical Support. In addition to a story line, you need to consider the support for learning and how to make it available. You still want your introduction, concept, and examples, and you may have job aids that are available when performing the task in the real world. These elements can remain external to the game or be brought into the game. For instance, you could have a reference library available in the game that the avatar can go to. Or you might have a character in the game tell a story about his or her experience, which can serve as an example.

For example, I've long had a design for an advertising literacy game (my personal set of games I'd like to do tend to hover around achieving meaningful social outcomes, the product of an overdeveloped social conscience I'm afraid). In the game, the character is in an advertising agency. I figured there would have to be a library of advertising campaigns in the past that could serve as examples, and a library of advertising design guidelines. In the game you could visit the office of an experienced character who would tell you a tale of a campaign (and could have a stack of them available to suit the state of the game).

It is important at this point to carefully consider the feedback upon the decision. Although it is still a matter of some debate about just *when* feedback should be given, there should be no debate that when the learner receives feedback, it should specifically refer to the framework and the learner's performance and yet remain believable in the context of the story. So some agent in the game, such as a supervisor, mentor, or even outraged recipient of inappropriate behavior on the part of the learner's character or avatar, should indicate how and why the learner's actions violated the principles of the underlying concept. For instance, a customer might point out to a sales avatar that because the character failed to properly research the customer's needs as good sales folk should, he or she is going to pursue the deal with a competitor of the company.

Note that a game might present a number of these series of decisions, thereby giving the player multiple chances at practice. You can make multiple linked or contingent scenarios with gradually increasing difficulty, or you can build into the engine the ability to generate essentially unlimited scenarios by pulling from a list of situation templates, populated randomly or programmatically from lists of character names or company names, or whatever. To really develop an important skill, you may want learners to have lots of practice, so creating a game that presents many examples and slowly allows the learners to achieve success over many iterations is possible and desirable.

One nice capability of the game engine approach is to have templates for several levels of problem difficulty (with simpler or more complex variables, for instance, or more or less work already done for you in the problem situation) and gradually increase the difficulty through rules. To achieve previously mentioned adaptive learning (and adaptive game play), you can tie how fast learners get harder problems to how well they perform.

You have to decide how much support to provide in terms of job aids. One of the steps in designing a learning solution is to determine when to create a job aid for performance in the real world. If you know learners can't have a job aid (and increasingly, with mobile devices and different modalities, this shouldn't be the case), you have to ensure that there is sufficient practice in the game to automate all the essential skills. If they will be able to use job aids in the real-world performance, then you should consider making them available in the game.

You also need to explicitly consider the nongame elements that surround the learning experience. You may not want to embed all the content within the game; driving learners to other resources, particularly discussion, is very valuable when mentors or discussion facilitators are available. If you design a game without considering how it's going to be part of the larger learning process, you won't design appropriately. I heard Shirley Alexander (pro-vice-chancellor at the University of Technology, Sydney, and a leading light in the use of technology for learning) use the phrase "learning ecosystem" in conversation at a conference, and that's a concept I think is useful for thinking about how games play a role in learning. So you should think that you're designing a learning ecosystem, and the game is just part of a larger picture from the learner's perspective, augmented by discussions, information resources, knowledge tests (yes, there's a role for them), and other elements.

A point taken from games is providing contextual help available at the point of need. In general, beyond a certain simple level in technology-mediated systems, you want to provide a help system. If there's not a referral to an available person (and as a first line of defense, even if there is), you'll want to consider providing a help capability.

One of the nice features of the linear or branching scenario is that you know exactly where learners are and can create appropriate content to be presented at those points if they have trouble. You can handcraft the help for those particular locations. In the case of a game engine, you'll have to take a templated approach to help just as you do to the decision. The decision is likely to be driven from a template that has an associated interface, and you can customize the help to that interface. Ideally, you'll also use the variable states populating the model to customize the feedback.

In the "Quest" game (Case Study 1 in Chapter Four), for instance, the game engine tracked the variables to see whether any was dangerously low (or high) and also to see whether learners had been searching enough. Feedback based upon this was available if they asked for help. We also monitored the variables on an ongoing basis to offer help proactively, but that was done deliberately because we wanted to avoid damaging self-esteem with the particular audience.

There can be two types of help. One is for the instructional task, and another is for the game interface. For learning, you may want to consider a layered design, where the first inquiry reveals just a tip, and subsequent queries provide more targeted help. You may also want a layered system for the interface help, where you first get specific help to the particular screen interface, and there may be access from there to a more general help system with both a keyword index and a table of contents mechanism to access (a search interface is also welcome). The broader the scope of your design, the more likely this is.

Map Learning to Interface. An important decision is how to represent the information and choices to the learner. Although this is not an interface design text (I've taught interface design, respect the skill set, and do recommend that

Donald Norman's book *The Design of Everyday Things* (1990) is a brilliant, yet short and easy-to-read book about how to design for usability. It has become a classic on designing for the way people actually think, and you will not look at the world in the same way again. I highly recommend it. As a follow-up, I also recommend his *Things That Make Us Smart* (1993), about designing systems to support our goals.

you have this skill on your team), there are some underlying principles unique to learning environments in general and games in particular.

The basic premise is to clearly represent the current state of the environment and map the learner's goal to the available options. In general, the learner should be presented with choices that delineate the decisions they may really have to make. If they're not just talking to people but also acting on the world, their interface actions should mimic their intentions. For example, if learners need to indicate how much to rotate a knob, they should have a knob to rotate, not have to type in an angle. Although pragmatic constraints may rein this in, it's the place to start.

The way information is presented to the learner is critical, too. Edward Tufte's principles of clean information design are relevant here, in terms of appropriate mapping of relative values to graphic representations (Tufte, 1990, 1997, 2001). Graphic design and information design play a role in effectively implementing the game.

One of the innovations we see in console games is quite relevant here. Good games provide a built-in tutorial about how to play the game by providing practice on the game mechanics. Part of this has to do with mappings of complex combinations of button-presses to arbitrary actions (for example, simultaneously pressing the B-button and Z-button is a horizontal sword slash, whereas the combination of the B-button and X-button is a vertical sword slash). If we have complex motor skills (perhaps drilling keystrokes in a software application training simulation), we should consider such an activity. In general, however, we'll have different learning problems. Sometimes, when we strip down the actions in the interface, the mapping between the interface actions can be somewhat arbitrary. You may want an introduction to the interface (ideally set in the game) or a lot of "unscored" practice before it counts.

For example, in a project management game, you had to click on the list of projects to select one, then you had to understand a complex table to determine whether the data were good or out of range, and if they were out of range you had to talk to the responsible character and deal appropriately with the character's personality type to gain cooperation to revise the data. In the story line, you had an intelligent PDA to help you with the task, which allowed us to simplify the task where we wanted to and retain calling on the player for the "important" decisions, so we developed a tutorial for the PDA that really was the tutorial for the game interface. In this way, we scaffolded the task through the device, made the device coherent with the theme, and thematically taught the player how to play.

Once you've created the story and interface, then you need a way to populate the game decisions. That's the next step.

Build the Model. For each level of implementation, there are different requirements. For the mini-scenario model and the linear scenario model, the decision story board is sufficient. For the contingent scenario model, however, you have to identify all the branches and how they connect until you have all moves from all possible decision points covered by a branch to another decision, a successful termination, or an unsuccessful termination ("You're dead, sucker!").

For the full game model, you have to do more. You need an underlying representation of the situations and the conditions under which they can occur. You or your SME has to describe the contingencies in a way that the game engine can be implemented. You may or may not do implementation (and this book is not about the production side), but the design team is responsible for stipulating the initial conditions, the relationships embodied in the underlying model that the game engine implements, the actions the user can take and the effect those have on the underlying representation, and conditions to check for to determine success or failure. A programmer may map your stipulations to rules or code, but you need to specify the conditions.

Sometimes the relationships are strictly quantitative and can be modeled in Excel or in a quantitative modeling environment such as Stella. Here you have formulas that relate the actions the player takes to numerical changes to the system, and running the numbers through the calculations indicates the outcome.

In other cases, the model may be more qualitative. You'll still need a way to model the state of the world and the consequences of player actions. A typical way to handle this is to have a set of rules that are evaluated after player actions. These need to be stated in the form of *algorithms,* deterministic ways to take a set of conditions and systematically react to them. Eventually these will get translated into program code, but a useful shortcut is a form of *pseudo-code,* a shorthand that is language-like in form but fairly specific in mechanism. For instance, indicating that the consequence of a bad user action will decrement their score by one decrement can be represented as: *if answer_wrong then user_score = user_score – user_score_change.*

We need to create the set of important variables to be initialized (*user_ score = 0, won = false, user_score_change = 1*), the changes to those variables when things happen (*if answer_right then user_score = user_score + user_score_change*), and the conditions under which the game ends (*if user_score ≥ 100 then finished = true and won = true; if user_score < 0 then finished = true and won = false*). We stipulate these conditions and also capture the options that will be available at each decision point and the consequences.

Capturing each decision point will create a list of the screens that need to be created where situations requiring decisions are presented. One of the common tools used is a *lookup table,* a table that lists the conditions under which a situation could happen along one axis, and the different decisions that could occur in another. For instance, we could have the following table (Table 6-2). In this case, as a customer service representative if we point the customer to a help page, it's not so damaging for a customer who's reasonably happy as it is for an unhappy customer, and similarly, the benefits of offering personal

Table 6-2. Score Adjustment Lookup Table.

User_Score_Change	Happy Customer	Angry Customer
Indicate location of help page	−1	−2
Offer personal help	+2	+1

help work even better for a happy customer (this may not be the way things actually work, it is just a hypothetical model).

Note that game design could suggest that such options might be countered by the effect on time taken shown in Table 6-3 to make the decision more consequential. Of course, then time would have to be a factor in the game (but it should be, as usually trade-offs in customer happiness are at the cost of speed of response).

Table 6-3. Time Adjustment Lookup Table.

Time_Counter_Change	Indicate Location of Help Page	Offer Personal Help
	+5	+30

Another trick is to populate various aspects of the game from a database randomly. Say that you have a situation in the game in which you have clients come to you. You can use some randomness to determine whether they come from manufacturing, financial, health, or other industries. You may need to check with your SME to determine how frequently that happens, and the game might randomly assign a problem to the client or make it specific to the client's industry.

For instance, if the problem the customer were bringing to the learner was an accounting issue, it might be relatively the same for all but the financial services industries. But if it were a type of IT security issue, such as a network intrusion, it might very much change depending on what industry (for instance, in financial someone is trying to perpetrate identity theft, in manufacturing the goal is industrial espionage, and so forth). Similarly, you can introduce some randomness by choosing the company name or character names from a database. For instance, you could have a whole list of potential names and randomly assign them to characters at the start of each game, or as the game calls up the need for a character, you could pull one from the database.

In the project management game that followed the linear scenario in Case Study 3 (Chapter Five), each project that was in the initial list, or was added as the game progressed, was populated by a set of rules. A project name was pulled randomly from the list (without replacement; that is, once it was used it wouldn't be used again). Associated with each project was a set of four possible scopes in increasing complexity (low, medium, high, and completely ridiculous), so we could have requests to increase, or needs to decrease, the scope. An initial scope was randomly assigned from the set. Estimated and actual budget and time numbers were calculated from a formula that randomly picked within a range that represented appropriate values in this story. (As a consequence, learner decisions and the game's internal calculations were dependent on the numbers generated.) Similarly, characters responsible for the four areas for each of the projects were assigned randomly from a pool, some normal, some with various forms of personality disorder. Thus, we allowed significant replay without any likelihood of encountering previously seen situations.

Remember that novelty helps engagement and keeps learners from feeling as though the situation is too deterministic. Similarly, it allows the generation of different situations continually, allowing replay, which further allows learners to play to their level of comfort with the educational outcomes.

In personal experience in design teams, we have repeatedly found that a useful way to capture and communicate the interactive experience is through the use of state or flow diagrams. These diagrams are used to capture and represent the different types of decisions or situations the learner can face and the consequences of their actions in terms of transitions to other situations or decisions (see Figure 6-5).

This particular representation is generic but indicative of the type of diagram you might create. You typically won't have all of your model in one

Figure 6-5. State Flow Chart.

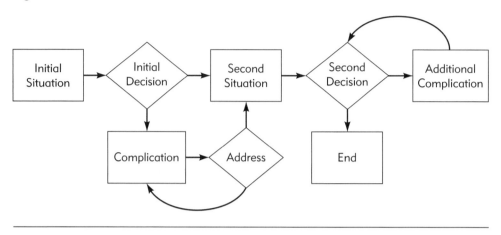

diagram, but will instead expand into more detailed descriptions certain components that are represented as boxes in the top-level diagram (the project management game that was the follow-on to Case Study 3 had five separate diagrams to capture the full interaction).

There are a variety of ways to provide the information to implement a game, but these are a few of the tools. To the extent that you think through the minimal number of variables, their initial values, the effects of actions to change those variables, and the ranges of those variables and values or combinations that trigger events including game end, you are providing the fodder for successful implementation.

Specify Outputs. The output of our specification phase has been ideally not only the specification of the prototype but also the questions the prototype should answer. Early on, it might be whether the setting should be the Wild West or a princess's castle, or whether a slider bar or a set of buttons representing ranges is more appropriate. The specification of the prototype might at this point be: Tell the users the situation, give them a goal and a paper mock-up of the interface, and ask what button they'd push. Later on we might have a full implementation with initial values, and the question might be how long the game takes to play at these settings.

In addition to the questions, the format of the output at some stage of iteration ideally is a *story board,* a specification of the game in terms of screen design, decision points, and perhaps any animations or movies used to bridge between game sections or represent the consequences of a decision. All the different types of screens should be there, including the beginning and introduction, any assistance screens or pedagogical support such as examples or job aids, and the types of screens that characterize the action. Not all screens need to be implemented, just all the types, and they need to be structured to represent the flow of the experience. It has to be enough to convey to a production team just what the game should look and feel like for implementation. You may graphically design the story board to convey a look and feel, or you may indicate a rough concept that a design team will take away to create the look and feel (in other words, these can be done serially or in parallel, depending on team makeup).

A story board is a minimal way to capture the game experience and communicate it, but for contingent scenarios the connections need to be indicated, and for model-based designs a *design document* (mentioned earlier) is needed. In game design teams, it's part of the communication to the financiers, as well as to team members. A design document incorporates the story board but also text descriptions of the interaction and captures the types of actions that happen through the underlying model so that it can be programmed. It can (and should) also include graphic design treatments. It should document the characters, variables, rules, probabilities, lookup tables, naming conventions, any timing issues, production notes, and so forth.

Implementation

The implementation stage is highly dependent on the quality of the output of the specification stage. If we have sufficiently stipulated the variables and necessary constants (to support tweaking parameters), been clear about the necessary rules, and documented the appropriate situations and choices that can be reached, we have a high likelihood of creating a viable implementation. You'll have to work with your implementation team to ensure that they have what they need to develop your design. I'm not talking about production here, however, so we'll move on.

Evaluation

We should have, from the design phase, a list of questions to be answered. Ideally, they're phrased in terms we can quantitatively measure. After ensuring that the prototype is robust enough for the current stage of development (no critical bugs, performance issues, or compatibility issues), we will get the usability issues out of the way first. Then we will evaluate the educational effectiveness, that is, whether the experience delivers the level of skill performance we need as an outcome. Finally, we will get to our engagement metrics.

Usability metrics are tested by giving the users certain goals and asking them to accomplish the goals through an interface. Our usability goals are fivefold: least time to accomplish a task, lowest time to learn to accomplish the task, greatest retention of the learning over time, lowest possible number of errors, and highest subjective evaluation of the experience. The goals typically avoid specifics of the interface—for example, "Click here to move on"— and instead focus on the cognitive goals of the users to see whether they can map goals (the ones you intend them to have) to the interface. So you should have goals such as "Review the sales order" or "Determine the current discrepancy between estimate and current cost."

Our educational metrics will be performance based and we will posttest sample users to see whether they have achieved our learning objectives. Generally, we test on ourselves at the beginning to get rid of coarse errors, then we use experts to get rid of well-known mistakes, and finally we test on sample users.

Engagement metrics are generally subjective, so that we ask the players how they like the game, how it compares to what they think could be done, or what worked and didn't. There are some quantitative measures, such as how much replay is observed, but in general I don't recommend going so far as measuring galvanic skin response (a measure of excitement). If it's commercial, we could see how much people are willing to pay, or even how far they'll go to play more. (Hey, a guy can dream!)

We will continue to refine the design, tuning the game experience, until we achieve the metrics we originally indicated were appropriate indicators. Of course, we may modify our metrics through experience. We typically find we were too ambitious, but it's not completely unknown to find that there's more that can be included than originally conceived.

Summary

The design of a game is a dynamic process that incorporates systematicity and creativity simultaneously. These are not mutually exclusive concepts. We are combining the steps of focusing on educational objective first (at the right level of application), but also understanding learners in ways beyond their knowledge levels. We are creating not only system performance and usability goals, but also educational and engagement goals we need to achieve. We are focusing on the proper setting for the decision skills and ensuring that the overall implementation aligns the theme with the learning goal, and then we're evaluating the outcome systematically to ensure it achieves those goals. The design process here is idealized, and there will be many adjustments made depending on context.

Summary Checklist

The checklist in Exhibit 6-4 supports the development process.

Exhibit 6-4. Game Design Checklist.

ANALYSIS
Ensure objective coached as skill.
Identify learner's existing knowledge.
Identify learner's motivations and interests
    Identify decisions
    Identify misconceptions
    Use analysis checklist (Exhibit 6.3)
Establish usability, education, and engagement metrics

SPECIFICATION
Situate the task in a model world
    Consider genre

Exhibit 6-4. Game Design Checklist, *Continued.*

Elaborate the details
   Adjust challenge
   Consider humor
   Plan media
   Incorporate randomness
   Develop characters
   Include misconceptions
   Include consequences
Incorporate pedagogical support
   Determine pedagogical surround
   Develop feedback
   Embed any concepts
   Embed any examples
   Embed any job aids
   Embed any help
Map learning to interface
   Communicate status
   Use good representations
   Consider embedding interface training
Build the model
   Establish variables
   Stipulate initial conditions
   Create rules that adjust values
   Identify terminal conditions
   Look for opportunities for novelty
Story-board the outcome

IMPLEMENTATION
Prototype

EVALUATION
Test usability
Test educational effectiveness
Test engagement

Set Design
and Afterthoughts

7

Pragmatics

ALTHOUGH THE DESIGN PROCESS stipulated in the previous chapter is a goal to shoot for, there are many ways in which the process can vary. Some of these can be anticipated, and there are some lessons learned that are worth reviewing. This chapter is a laundry list of thoughts and lessons learned about the pragmatic side of learning game design and development.

Budget

One of the biggest barriers in choosing a game approach, particularly an engine-driven game, typically is perception of a high cost. And to be fair, a game approach can be more expensive. Developing the underlying programming for a game engine brings in software development costs. There are several ways around this but also several arguments about why programming for a game engine may make sense anyway.

The first point is that sometimes you can justify the budget. If the skill is absolutely critical to the business, corners should not be cut on making the most effective learning experience. It also makes sense if you have a large audience to amortize the cost. For a critical accounting procedure that goes to a global audience of consultants, a $2 million budget may be justified.

Note that a $2 million budget, however, isn't necessary. I've developed a game on behalf of a client where the total cost to their client was around $100,000. Various factors will make this more or less, but the costs are dropping as tools get more powerful and our understanding is honed. LearningMate has created a process that produces engine-driven learning simulations (they call them scenarios) for substantially less than that (an order of magnitude).

Another factor to consider is that if you do a lot of thinking up front, you can remove much of the need for production values. I've created games with very simple interfaces and tools (see Case Study 1 in Chapter Four, for example). I've found that if the cognitive challenge is sufficient, the game is engaging and effective regardless of the "window-dressing." One of the factors that tends to drive up the cost is video and animation. However, with static screens, stock photos or simple graphics (research suggests underemphasizing ancillary media) can do a lot. So spend time and thought ensuring the right mental challenge, and you'll find that you need to do little else to make the experience engaging.

And, of course, you don't always need a full game engine, as indicated in Chapter Five. You can choose one of the other approaches: mini-scenarios, linked scenarios, or contingent scenarios—or any combination thereof. In one instance I created scenarios that were mostly linear but with some contingencies to allow some replay and experimentation. I created two of them in increasing difficulty (actually three; whereas the first one covered the whole process in a simplified form, the second, more detailed pass at the process was broken into halves in separate scenarios).

If you don't need to really drill the skill, these scenarios make sense; they are little more work than traditional instructional design, and they can be done with hard-coding of HTML links and not require any particular difficulty. In addition, tools are available to make these scenarios (Knowledge

Anywhere "rolled their own" tool after I kept pushing them to use contingent scenarios).

In Case Study 4 (Chapter Five), a relatively rich branching structure was written by the project manager (also a technical writer), and mostly in text with a few stock photos. The scenario was well received by the audience, since the overall experience was challenging and believable. As mentioned, your performance on a subsequent questionnaire depended on the information you got only if you made good choices.

Production

More and more people are working on tools to make game engines easy. As mentioned above, one of my clients developed a process and tools to produce game engines reliably, repeatedly, scalably, and cost effectively. Similarly, a colleague has built tools in Flash to make particular kinds of simulations easy. As groups continue to experiment and explore, we get increasingly better tools. Good tools help you bring down the cost.

Certain tools are designed to do particular things well. There are simulators available that make it particularly easy to develop interpersonal scenarios. There are other tools that make it easy to develop software simulations. And then there are professional game tools that let you develop professional-level games, with all that implies: heavier learning curves, commercial licenses, and real power.

You may consider being eclectic. HyperCard used to be a great prototyping tool and even a full game development environment. The classic game "Myst" was created in HyperCard, and I've developed several games in HyperCard as well. There are new programs similar to HyperCard that are cross-platform and should be easy to use. Visual Basic is a fairly easy and powerful environment and is certainly valuable for the PC world. A new tool is Squeak. Based on the language Smalltalk, and led by the brilliant Alan Kay, the Squeak team is creating Squeak as an environment for kids to learn programming through games. It's available on lots of platforms and could become a very useful tool.

Marc Prensky (2000) has recognized that commercial games are increasingly providing the capability to produce *mods,* or modifications, of the games. He suggests that you can use these as your game development environment. For example, you could model your workspace in a first-person shooter environment (for example, "Doom" or "Quake") and then allow people to navigate around and get familiar with the layout—or, more important, populate it with safety problems that need to be fixed.

A word of caution: I think it's a mistake to shoehorn a learning game into a commercial game if you have to compromise your learning objectives. The focus has to be on the learning objective first. If you can do so, however, even though it's still difficult (get someone experienced, like a kid), it's a very powerful environment.

Increasingly, however, Flash is becoming *the* tool for the job. It's small, it now comes installed in most browsers, and it supports graphics and coding. I've had full games developed in Flash, such as the project management game that was the follow-up project to Case Study 3 (in Chapter Five).

Flash should be capable for small games, which is most of what I expect to get developed. If you've managed to secure the resources, there are professional-level tools. Panda 3D is an open source tool to create real 3D games. Developed originally at Disney, it is now being supported at Carnegie Mellon University. If you're going to do a major project (or projects), it may be a worthwhile investment to get your programming team up to speed on such a real tool. At the time of writing, it has all the benefits and downsides of open source: you can use it and beat on it as you wish, but the support is eclectic. Still, it's a real tool, with real power and real opportunity.

Prototyping Tools

Another important consideration is your prototyping equipment. I can't emphasize enough how important it is to use the lowest-cost tool you can to get your answers early in the process. If you discover you've been going down the wrong path (and you will), it's much harder to change if you've invested too soon in high production.

Long ago I advocated the Double Double P's: postpone programming, and prefer paper. Rob Phillips, then at Curtin University's multimedia group, led me to this when he made me aware of his team's rule that they don't put a finger to keyboard until the entire program has been designed on paper. Paper is inexpensive, easy to modify, and easy to throw away. It was a great insight.

Paper can be used in lots of ways. The Pictive technique for interface design uses scraps of paper to represent interface widgets (different elements, such as sliders, buttons, text fields, and graphic fields) and lets you experiment with different interfaces by recombining the elements (Muller, 1993). You can show what happens by having users point to what they'd do, and replace the appropriate portion of the "screen" with the appropriate new bit of paper. Rob Moser (2000), in his Ph.D. thesis, prototyped his game on paper by creating pages that represented each place you could get to. He then tested the design by showing players the page they were on and indicating the available options. He let players know where they were and what had happened by showing them where they had arrived as a result, or a different page showing how things had changed. You can also do things like testing people's preferences in labels for actions and things by having different terms on different slips of paper, have players group them, and then create an overall label for the group. The HCI field has developed a substantial body of work on using paper to prototype.

Another prototyping tool is Microsoft's PowerPoint application (or any other such presentation tool). With it, you can easily mock up screens and have screen clicks that take you to other screens. Thus, you can easily prototype the user experience. PowerPoint is easy to learn and is ubiquitous, so it's unlikely to be an expensive solution.

And, of course, there's HTML. Using a tool like DreamWeaver, and HTML tables, you can mock up screens and have links take you between the screens to create, like in PowerPoint, a usable experience. One advantage of HTML is that you can easily make the prototype broadly available, and with some background *instrumenting* (creating programmatic hooks that will record a user's actions) you can track different people's usage of the prototype. Talk to your Web developers or tech support about this.

Note that once you've nailed down your environment and design, it then makes sense to get your environment up and running quickly. The fact that you need to tune suggests that you need a working implementation in order to tune. And you should be iterating a lot. Contrary to my position on postponing programming, John Hathaway, chief learning technologist of GeneEd, advocates early development of the programming environment to support the tuning process. He's working in Flash, which makes it easy to get code up and running. My concern is that there is a great potential to go into hard coding of the rules and consequent difficulty tuning. As long as you have software engineers who understand programming, and they make it easy to modify and change the variables through good design, this can make sense.

I now believe that you should postpone programming until you have settled on the general design of your solution, and you should do that early. Then get a shell up that's developed modularly that allows you to tune to the final design. Note that if you design for reusability, you may be able to amortize the development investment across different problems. It may well be that we'll have Flash tool sets oriented toward different types of activities by the time you read this.

Media

It can appear that there is a conflict between the recommendation to keep media educationally focused and the desire to establish theme. Media merely to add the proverbial bells and whistles are unnecessary (or worse), but ones that help establish the theme and story are appropriate. To discriminate, it helps to review the roles of media.

For principled reasons, I like to use media according to the properties they convey. Thus, I break up media into categories by determining whether they're static or dynamic and whether they're linguistic or visual. Within the latter, I determine whether they're emphasizing the context or the concept (see Table 7-1).

Table 7-1. Properties of Media.

	Static	Dynamic
Contextual	Photos	Video
Conceptual	Graphics	Animation
Languistic	Text	Audio

When the necessary information is inherently changing, particularly in a continual fashion, dynamic media are appropriate. In other situations, static media are sufficient. What I mean by contextual is showing the actual context, such as photographs, versus an abstraction (conceptual). In general, dynamic media are more expensive than static media, so I suggest aiming for static unless you need the dynamic.

One constraint on dynamic media is that if learners' attention is distracted (and this can happen for a variety of reasons: a phone call, a visit, or knocking over a drink), they can miss some of the dynamic media. For that reason, I advocate putting controls on any dynamic media (unless paying attention is part of the objective). At a minimum, allow the learner to click on the representation to restart (an implicit control), but ideally have controls for play, pause, and so forth available.

I'm a big fan of conceptual graphics, because that's the way I think (as you may infer from the graphics in Chapter Five). I have to be pushed into remembering to make things concrete. Others are the reverse. Some situations naturally benefit from one or the other, but different learners will benefit from different presentations. This is one way in which the goal of creating different representations can be addressed. In general, it may make sense to emphasize concepts in the concept section of the learning, and use context to illustrate examples and contextualize practice. Cartoons and comics are an interesting way to bridge the two (discussed later). Another approach I've seen that is interesting and potentially powerful is to lay the concept over the context (line graphics of conceptual models laid over a photo, for instance) or even provide the ability to switch between the concept and the context or show both.

The first principle on the use of media is to only add what is essential to learning. We typically do not go far enough to use graphics to communicate relationships, tables to help communicate data, or photos to contextualize performance. However, it's possible to overdo it. Media also require some of the available cognitive processing capacity. That has to be weighed in the larger context of the task you are asking the learner to perform. Ruth Clark and Richard Mayer (2003) recite some research that, carefully qualified, gives guidelines about the appropriate use of media.

If the media don't interfere by requiring extra cognitive capacity to process, or as a strategy to increase challenge we *want* to increase cognitive load, we can consider using media but only if the media assist in the learning task or engagement. Any other use is proscribed. The point is that there are costs not only in production, but also in cognitive processing capability, and costs need to be carefully evaluated.

When it comes to creating graphics, we know some specifics. We know we should integrate text into the diagram (Chandler & Sweller, 1991). We know we should eliminate excess graphics. We know that dynamic media make it difficult to process any adjacent static media (for example, the dreaded flashing Web graphic). We know that if there is some dynamic medium, there should be a way to control it and view it again in case our attention was taken away.

We also know that there are times when dynamic media are the most effective communication media. When necessary, we should use them. Video and audio clips of people can establish context very well. It's often the case that you can get relevant people to play roles in your stories or tell relevant stories to make the concept accessible. Dynamic consequences can most effectively be communicated through dynamic media. However, consider when they are really needed. If it's a dynamic event with discrete steps, a series of static images may be an acceptable, or even desirable, trade-off. Even for procedures in which one step follows another, whereas video is preferable, consecutive, still images will work. Similarly, with graphics versus animation, a series of still graphics can replace an animation if you are capturing a series of discrete steps, although an animation might be preferable.

By the way, this breakdown discusses audio solely for the spoken word, but there are other audio uses such as music or noises. What is less clear is how to characterize them. Background music, in general, can set the mood, both thematically and to support particular approaches (for example, to ramp up energy when the task is motor or to slow down when the task is reflective). Some people may find it annoying, and you might want to have a setting to turn it off. Noises from machinery may be part of the context or a clue about changes in the world. Consider, as above, the benefits versus the costs.

Writing

One form of media is writing. Most people figure they know how to write, but there are many different styles of writing and not all are appropriate. It's surprising how often people will pay for professional graphic designers and programmers, but will let anyone write the prose or, even worse, dialogue.

In Case Study 2, I mention how a comedy skit writer reliably and repeatedly took my well-crafted paragraphs and boiled them down to two sentences. The point is that to ignore professionalism in the writing can have as much impact on the user experience as lack of professionalism in other areas—particularly when you're doing some of the scenario modes and trying to keep costs down.

Professional creative writers are experienced in setting moods, writing dialogue, and so forth. However, they may not be knowledgeable about interactive experiences. Game designers may be the reverse. Note that one person doesn't have to be in charge of all such components, and you may want to have someone (for example, yourself) responsible for the interactive design but bring in professional writers for text and dialogue.

Humor

Another point to consider that came from my experience with the scriptwriter is the difficulty of using humor. In general, humor is a good idea—and it is underused. However, it is also hard to do well.

John Cleese's humorous training videos are legendary, but achieving that level of humor is more difficult than it looks. Unless you have a trained comic skit writer handy, you should err on the side of caution and test your ideas. Knowing your audience is a good guide. Microsoft created the Crabby Office Lady as a sarcastic help function (Bob's evil twin?), but it works since it is honest and occasionally funny, and the audience appreciates that sometimes technical things can be stupid.

I've used bad puns in names for characters, things, and places (Giva Dam is one of my more egregious examples). I've also had some silly setups (a character being gulled into interplanetary service by promising advertisements, but the real job was more mundane). In other cases, I eschewed humor, either due to the nature of the material, the audience, or because the client insisted.

It doesn't have to be all comic, or all dramatic, either. For instance, even dramatic movies may have bits of humor (remember "Snakes, why did it have to be snakes?" from *Raiders of the Lost Ark*?). Similarly, comedies have a dramatic story that underpins the jokes, such as saving lives in *M*A*S*H*.

I encourage you to consider and try humor. I also suggest you test it out before making it final. Humor is a valuable but delicate thing.

Cartoons and Comics

One way humor is expressed in culture is through cartoons and comic strips. However, comic strips and cartoons are also valuable teaching tools for a variety of reasons. One of the reasons that is not conceptually pure but very pragmatic is that the medium has inherently low bandwidth requirements. The simple lines and colors compress well, making them quick to download.

One of the reasons to consider comics is that we're well acculturated to parse comic books. We generally have lots of experience in comprehending them, and that is a valuable commodity. Comic books can strip away unessential details, emphasize particular aspects, and include humor. They're great for providing examples.

Another reason, as mentioned in Case Study 2, is that the thought bubbles in cartoons, like voice-overs, are a great way to communicate the underlying thought processes that experts tend to forget to articulate. Alan Shoenfeld's work, as discussed in talking about Cognitive Apprenticeship in Chapter Two of this book, has identified underlying thought processes as important components in helping learners understand the alternatives that could be considered at each stage of a problem-solving process, and thus they really help deliver the promise of modeled examples.

As discussed under the Media section in this chapter, comics are also a unique combination of context and concept. Like a game or simulation, comics are a stripped-down context that helps emphasize the concepts, but they are set in a world that doesn't fully convey any one specific context. Comics point to our experience in a way that lets us fill in the gaps for our own context. This may be a key to their power for communication.

You may not go so far as Scott McCloud (1993) and call comics "art" (though I personally think *Calvin & Hobbes* was true genius, and *Bloom County* and *Doonesbury* are every bit works of art), but the value for communication and education is undeniable. I do recommend you get someone with a true grasp of the form. In my experience, I've found that I can stipulate a concept and one representation of it, and a good artist can either render it or come up with a better way to capture the same concept.

Culture

One of the issues that may create a barrier for the use of games is the culture of the audience. Research has shown that computer-game playing in different cultures is driven by and satisfies different needs, and games that are a hit in one country may not be so in another. Similarly, humor varies significantly by culture. Even learning styles may have correlates in cultural differences. Consequently, we would expect that computer games for learning might be constrained by cultural boundaries.

If we're designing for a broader audience, for instance a global training staff or a culturally diverse educational institution, we need to consider culture explicitly. As long as the learning goals are relevant to the culture, we can consider games as a training vehicle. What will be likely to change are the thematic setting and characters we might use. We may want to make them less culturally identified or more culturally diverse.

What we don't want are culturally specific situations (unless they represent our learning goal), but instead ones that are appropriate across the cultures of our audience. So, for instance, in a business software–selling scenario, we worked to make sure that the business decision was generic enough and the characters' names were of enough varied ethnicity that they weren't obviously from the United States (where the scenario was authored). If the situations *are* culture-specific (a globally mobile team with clients in many countries, say), we might need to create a mix of situations across the cultures our audience needs to address. In this case, we might have negotiations that vary depending on the country in which the negotiations are conducted.

A more appropriate but more time-consuming approach is to make culture-specific versions of the games. This is the same approach taken with software when software is internationalized (localization is much more efficient when the original content is first optimized to be localized, a process called internationalization) and then localized. Here, you identify the parts of the game that will be adapted, such as dialogue, text, or culturally specific graphics. You also may separate out labels in graphics onto separate layers, tag sections of content, and place dialogue on separate tracks from music and video. Then you create separate versions of the materials that need to be changed for each culture.

The localized version is the ideal, as many would argue that you could not make a culture-neutral version. I'd suggest that you can use the organizational culture, but depending on the circumstances, localization may be more appropriate.

Gender

Another issue is gender. This issue appears in several ways in games, in that you may want to ensure that you have an appropriate mix of genders for characters and choose game genres that appeal to the genders of your audience.

Some of the research into the gender issue has converged on an opinion that guys like "twitch" games, ones that require motor skills, whereas gals like social activities in their games. My first response is that the educational goal has to drive the action (though settings can change). I also believe, as stated elsewhere in the book, that if it's a cognitive challenge, both genders will find it engaging. However, you should consider the gender mix of the audience if you're developing learning. If you're working with all-male sports teams, you might take a different approach to sexual-harassment training than you might with mixed-gender company, for instance. This is increasingly an unlikely situation, however.

Another thing I often do is to choose character names and dialogues that are not gender-specific. For example, Chris, Tracy, and Pat are English names that can be either male or female. There are lists of such names on the Web, at least for English names.

Age and Development

Age and, more accurately, developmental level is an issue that has not been addressed here. The assumption has been that you're developing for adult audiences. There are certain adaptations that have to be made when developing for kids. In addition to knowledge levels (kids just haven't had so much life experience), there are other factors to consider.

Up until about age thirteen or so, kids have limitations on their cognitive ability. Jean Piaget identified several levels of capability, and subsequent research has shown that in totally abstract terms those levels hold up, though with support learners can do more. Younger kids have less working memory capacity (how many things they can hold in their head), they may not be able to work on two dimensions at once (color and size, for instance; before a certain age it's likely that they can only deal with one at a time), and their motor skills, both coarse and fine, are less developed. They also have different interests. Their preferences in music, colors, and amount of required variety differ. What they find interesting and funny will be different.

If you are designing for kids, I first suggest you get a developmental psychologist on your team who understands children's cognitive capabilities, or a designer who has a developmental background. You need professional guidance on this, and you can't just look it up (I qualified in developmental psychology and *I* wouldn't trust me). Second, I recommend you get kids participating in the design, and plan on lots of user testing. Kids are great (I have two myself) and designing for them can be incredibly rewarding, but it's easy to get it wrong. Do it right.

Evaluation

In evaluation, the ideal path is to get real users, test with them to get objective data, and then talk with them to get subjective data, using sufficient subjects to get statistical validity. Because that is often implausible, it's worth knowing some alternate approaches.

I've suggested before how the usability-HCI field has made advances ahead of educational technology. In addition to prototyping tools, the field has developed some testing approaches. Jakob Nielsen (1994) has developed an approach that he calls "heuristic evaluation." His data suggest that you catch 80 percent of the usability problems with five users. That is a pretty small number. Although there is some controversy about this, the point is that a small set of subjects (for example, five to seven) can be a valuable set, instead of the twenty or so you might need for statistical significance.

I also believe that early on in the development process you can use less-representative users and save the harder-to-acquire audience for final testing, if obtaining your target audience is expensive or difficult. Start with yourself and your team to get gross errors out of the way, then progress to other folks nearby who are not part of the development team but are available (nearby administrative staff, for example), and then get representative users from within your organization. If you are developing for an external audience, you'll want to reserve your time and money for externally representative audiences until near the end of the developmental cycle.

I also recommend mixing in some expert evaluation with user testing. Yes, you may have to pay experts (if you don't have usability or instructional design expertise outside of your group in the organization), but instead of just identifying the problems, they can also recommend solutions. Start with usability expertise (as mentioned earlier, you have to get usability problems out of the way first), then instructional expertise. Game advice is harder, though you can get experienced game industry or learning game expertise. However, the best way to fine-tune is through your users.

I do recommend bringing in advice early. It's much harder to change direction after substantial resources are invested. In Chapter Six, I mentioned a situation when I recommended a change to a game such that random events would be caused by side effects, not a character's inconsistent whims. Frankly, the client agreed, but they were too far down the production path to make the change!

Multiplayer Games

An increasing phenomenon is the multiplayer game. There are two main types: (1) games where small groups play different roles and compete or cooperate to accomplish goals and (2) the so-called massively multiplayer online games (MMOGs; for example, "EverQuest"), where large numbers of people interact in communities. Although the large environments of MMOGs have complicated support for economies and status, people eventually work together in smaller groups, so the focus here will be on small groups. Note that many (including two reviewers of the book) think that MMOGs have a lot of potential for learning in the future. Once we have more intelligent software agents (not *much* more is needed) and massive persistent worlds that have lots of educational opportunities, we may be able to set up situations where learning can occur, much as Montessori schools work now.

There are reasons to work in groups: so a group shares a behavioral change or revelation, so individuals can learn to work together as a group, or if the required skill set is distributed across roles. One addition is that you need to provide ways to communicate. You'll also have to determine whether there are fixed roles (easier) or whether you want to allow any number to join in a modeled environment.

Another pragmatic consideration is that your game design could have a role that is very hard to model, such as a journalist asking questions. In this case, it might make sense to have another person play the role in the game. (Neal Stephenson's [1996] brilliant "The Diamond Age" had a learning device positioned in the future that recruited actors to role play in the games it used to educate a child.)

In a sense, the criteria for a group game should come from your educational goals, so if your goals so dictate, you can develop a learning game to accommodate. The design process as stipulated should account for the multiple players. By the way, group games are likely to require group members to be available synchronously, and that removes some of the advantages of providing e-learning games.

Nonelectronic Games and Electronic Interactions

This book is specifically about e-learning games, but the principles discussed hold for other forms of learning games as well. In the research for this work, I've looked at many forms of entertainment. Although not an expert on live training games, I did peruse some works of Thiagi (Thiagarajan, 2003), the guru of learning games. His principles are similar to the elements I've identified in Chapter Three for creating engagement, although he allows much more freedom to interpret, as his designs are for human facilitators (that is an ideal situation in many cases, particularly when the knowledge is less well-defined).

One caveat here is that live learning games require additional skills in group motivation and control that are extraneous to the game, and are not covered here. The principles here may assist you in designing the activity, but they won't necessarily help you in running it! The spontaneity of live learning games is a wonderful thing, but not something we are yet able to reproduce. However, our capabilities continue to grow, and we should think to the future.

The principles also apply to the field known as interaction design or experience design. Creating a compelling experience is increasingly considered a differentiator for electronic environments as part of the goal of achieving customer loyalty. Using these principles should help address engagement while achieving marketing goals. After all, good marketing is really customer education.

Technology Environments

On the topic of the technology environment (or lack thereof), it is worth considering how such games would be registered with a Learning Management System (LMS) or Learning Content Management System (LCMS). (I'll refer to LMS as the generic category.) Such systems typically track learning as part of a larger aim of assessing and developing individuals according to long-term learning goals.

One of the considerations of designing a learning game should be considering any constraints in terms of being launched by an LMS, and eventually reporting the results back. Technically, this should not be a problem. If you're developing for a particular LMS, the technical implementation will just have to use a particular Application Program Interface (API) to accomplish those goals. If the solution may have to work across different LMSs, there are now standards (SCORM, or Standard Content Object Reference Model, stipulated by the Advanced Distributed Learning initiative of the U.S. Department of Defense, is the major one) that you could design to and have a good chance that most major LMSs would accommodate it.

One of the advantages of games as environments for practice is the potential use as formative and summative evaluation environments. To the extent that we have developed authentic practice, we have the basis for authentic evaluation. With our environment, we have the capability of recording behavior, and with our design we have real skills. But we have one qualification, in that we may not have a comparable experience. How do we cope?

First, remember that we're designing to well-specified performance objectives. We should have criteria and be able to test them. Certainly we can test independently of the learning environment as well, in the usual fashion, but we also have performance happening in the environment. With some assumptions, we can use that performance to the learner's benefit.

Given that the assumption here is that we have an e-learning implementation, we certainly have the capability of tracking performance. We can instrument the model to track performance and report it to the learner, or even to the LMS.

The difficulty really comes from how you indicate a score or success. With mini-scenarios and pure linear scenarios, you can score just like a multiple-choice question or a quiz. However, with contingent scenarios or game engines it's likely that players will not see the same questions.

For contingent scenarios you can have points attached to different branches and record the total score. However, the real point is to ensure that the learner achieve a certain level of performance. With contingent scenarios you can require that learners play again until they achieve a certain score. With games, you can make the success rules such that learners can't finish until they achieve a certain level of performance. Or you can create rules giving them only a certain number of chances. Of course, you can always provide a subsequent assessment as well. Or you can provide a fixed sequence for the assessment.

These performances can be separate from the formative evaluation, or they can be both formative and summative. They can also be part of portfolios of performance (which give a richer picture of the learner's capabilities) that can include performance on knowledge tests, interviews, 360-degree assessment, and so forth.

One of the neat things about contingent scenarios and games is that since learners can take different paths, if you record and represent the paths, you have a natural tool for discussion and reflection with the learner. Keeping a record of the learner's actions, particularly in a concise and illustrative representation, offers real hope for a learning ecosystem that incorporates mentors or discussion facilitators (or even peers, if you can generate a trusted learning environment with a focus on improvement, not on assessment).

Teams and Talent

As a final pragmatic concept, I want to emphasize the importance of designing in a group. There are a couple of reasons that having more than one person is good. First, there is a greater pool of potential input and ideas. Research shows that the outcome of a group can be better than that of the best individual of the group. Second, you can carve up the expertise. The task of designing a game integrates many disciplines: instruction, software, and all the incorporated media (writing, graphics, perhaps video or audio capture, and animation), as well as the project management. It's not only too much to expect one person to have all the necessary skills, it is a mistake to not get all the expertise required.

Having a diversity of personalities can also be a potential problem, since managing diverse agendas, egos, and languages can be challenging. Different fields use different languages (hence the efforts of Chapters Two and Three to lay out the fields of learning and engagement separately and then Chapter Four to create an alignment); individuals in one field may misinterpret statements of individuals from another field. And the recommendations from two areas, for sound reasons, may contradict one another. What do you do when the graphic designer and the software engineer disagree? I have found that having one person being ultimately responsible for the design, and consequently having ultimate control of the decisions, is the way to go. That person, of course, should have an understanding of the principles presented here.

In usability design, adherents of an approach called *participatory* design advocate including representatives of your audience on your design team.

William Goldman (screen writer for *Butch Cassidy and the Sundance Kid*, among many notable other films) brilliantly illustrates the benefits of having a team approach in his classic book *Adventures in the Screen Trade* (1989). He asks a cinematographer, director, composer, and other representatives from the movie-making process to review a sample screenplay that he has written, and he documents the resulting feedback from them and how he would change the concept.

Although few would disagree that your testing should use a representative sample of your audience, this approach goes further and suggests having them participate in the design. The advantages are that you have subject matter expertise built into the team. It has also been a fairly reliable situation that as you develop increased functionality, your audience changes in the sense that its understanding of the possibilities and new opportunities evolves (hence the *underengineering* and *extreme programming* movements that emphasize rapid prototyping and iteration). Thus, having members along can allow you to capitalize on that development. However, it can often be difficult to free up your audience from their regular tasks, so although it's worth considering, you also have to justify the benefit in comparison to the costs.

By the way, working together is more difficult when the groups are dispersed. It's properly a tight cycle of design, and you need contributions from all team members. I have had experiences working with a production team (graphics and programming) that was distant, and the distant team was more reactive than proactive. The design suffered as a consequence. I think that an initial meeting face to face, at least, is desirable to establish some camaraderie and to smooth subsequent rough times. The specification stage in particular works best when all the skills are represented and participating actively. Given the iterative nature of designing and tuning, the specification phase isn't discrete, and being dispersed may be more of a problem than in other design tasks.

What are the necessary skills? In some sense, it depends on the level of the project. You clearly need someone who understands learning and someone who has some creativity and talent for engagement. Project management is a key addition. Some production capability, such as the ability to code Web pages, is also usually the starting point. And you need some media skills. You can often find the above in two people, an instructional designer and a programmer. When you go beyond stock photos or clip art as media (and picking them isn't necessarily for the amateur), you'll need your media experts. Graphic design is usually a minimum to get a reasonable-looking screen design. Of course, as you ramp up the production quality, you'll need interface design, experts in all media incorporated (audio, video, animation, and so forth), programmers and software engineers, and more. And SMEs.

When you make the jump to contingent scenarios, and definitely for a game engine, you need a new, non-obvious skill: the ability to visualize the interaction *space,* all the possible paths and experiences that flow out of a model. There's a design tactic of bouncing between a model and a resulting experience, which you essentially "run" mentally, that gives you your initial system. And this is a developed skill. A concomitant but not necessarily identical skill is the ability to take a desired experience and map it into rules, as I talked about in Chapter Six. (Deborah Zimmerman, from Case Study 5, convinced me that having both is an unusual combination.) The skills that allow you to create a compelling experience and the ones that let you stipulate the variables and rules are not necessarily the same skills. Note that having two people with these skills together is not sufficient; they must also have a way to talk to one another. It's not magic, I believe it's trainable, but it's not obvious either, and you should not trust it to happen. You need to engineer it through having a framework to align the thought processes.

Ultimately, the success of the design and the project depends on getting a shared vision about what the experience will do, getting contributions from the members, and guiding those contributions to the desired ends. It's the leadership, not surprisingly, as well as the process that leads to a successful design.

8

Future Issues

S O FAR, I've been talking about the now, about the doable, but it's also important to be prepared for the future. There are a number of directions that are becoming increasingly important, and I think it's worthwhile to discuss them. There's some really interesting stuff coming, too!

Affect

Donald Norman (2003), in his book *Emotional Design,* has augmented his emphasis on designing for how people think to include considering people's emotions. His argument is that aesthetics matter, as I mentioned in the first chapter, an argument that supports the premise of this book. But it also implies that our design process needs to look for an aesthetic. That is what we do when aligning elements to communicate theme. It also suggests professionalism in all the components. Also, the process of user testing and tuning is designed to create an overall aesthetically appealing experience.

The more interesting point, however, is the implication for learning. One of Norman's points is that *affect,* the emotional experience, has an impact on how we process information. He points to research that suggests that positive affect leads to broader processing, and negative affect leads to deeper processing. Put another way, if the experience is positive, we tend to bring in more associations (but perhaps miss some details). But if the experience is negative, we tend to dig deeper, perhaps missing some connections. He provides lists of things that create positive affect (soft, warm, soothing) and negative affect (harsh, bitter, cacophonous).

If emotions do indeed affect learning, we may consider adapting the atmosphere appropriately. For instance, we may start with a positive affect to help the learner make connections, but then by raising the tension through drama and challenge we may help the learner process more deeply to get into the nuances of the skill. This emotional aspect may also be a consequence of game and challenge, and naturally suggest another reason games are more effective for learning.

I hope that there will be some fundamental research on this in the future, perhaps a Ph.D. topic for some bright student.

Learning Objects

A movement that is gaining strength, while wrestling with some difficulties, is the move to standards for learning technology and the concept of *learning objects*. The notion is that learning content can be divided into small independent units, or objects. These units can be distributed and tracked independently, providing for some technological benefits. One benefit has been argued to be that these learning objects can be reused and combined in new ways, or repurposed to different needs easily, so that an "example" content object might not only be part of a learning experience, but might be delivered to assist in a performance example. Or, an example about sales contract negotiation might serve both sales training and negotiation training. I have also argued that with very specific constraints on size, scope, and purpose, they can be intelligently sequenced (by the system) to create personalized learning, so that one learner might get an example first, another a concept first.

One of the controversies about learning objects is whether they can truly be independent or whether they are inherently context-specific. The view is that at best we can have information objects, and until combined in a particular context they don't constitute learning objects unless the size of the object is a whole course, which essentially precludes any benefit to a model other than a learning management system. For instance, if we have a "concept" object, by itself it might not lead to learning unless it was delivered in a performance context where the individual faces a problem, so that the concept object was a relevant framework for addressing the immediate problem in the context and consequently helps link the concept and the problem.

Games are inherently contextual, as we spend so much effort to create the context (read: theme) to make the decisions meaningful, which argues strongly for the context-specific view. However, there are benefits to learning object standards. I've wrestled with the conflict for some time, having argued for learning objects and also being an advocate of games for learning. Although the simple answer is to package the whole game as an object, there is another approach.

I believe that the learning objects should be "wrapped" in the game surrounding. Each decision is a practice object, and the underlying template for the decision may be extractable as a problem generator. The job aids, concepts, and examples built into the game can technically be considered learning objects. I would suggest making them available externally from the game and accessible to learners. For example, in analyzing the task and the performance objective, a job aid might be indicated, and that job aid could be made available both in the game and through a company information portal for access after the learning experience. This suggests designing learning objects from the beginning to be useful to tasks outside the game. But that's just a good idea anyway.

Going Mobile

Another new trend is the increasing use of mobile devices for learning (another area where I've been a spokesperson). Portability is a recognized component, but also user-triggered access and other capabilities are around the corner. One such capability is context awareness, knowing where the user is and customizing learning appropriately. Other considerations include the different media involved, when and how to use audio from a mobile phone or screen from a PDA, and different ways to provide feedback.

One of the obvious solutions is to make interactive learning games available through a mobile device: a laptop, PDA, or phone. To the extent that these devices are always connected and include a browser, with any appropriately composed Web page learning can be anywhere and anytime. Another approach is to use a widely available environment. As yet, however, not all devices have Flash, so you may be constrained in the solutions you can use (such as Java) or you may need proprietary ones (such as Qualcomm's BREW software development environment for mobile phones and some other devices). A small scenario could work on a mobile phone, even using the phone's audio for the dialogue or mimicking a phone call.

Making available games that take advantage of the location is a second opportunity. Such a game might require information in the environment, so you'd have to look around a device or location to find some information, which could be a tool to familiarize yourself with an environment or system. Such games have been done for entertainment and certainly could be extended to learning games.

An appropriately composed Web page, by the way, is a Web page written in a language that separates content from form, such as eXtensible Markup Language (XML), with a customized specification for delivery through a Document Type Definition (DTD).

One of the underexplored areas of mobile learning is using mobile devices to spread learning over a longer time by dribbling content, examples, and practice in smaller chunks over an extended period. We know this leads to better retention, but we often cannot engineer such situations. However, with mobile devices we can.

A new opportunity to address this capability for persistent learning comes from some games that have been developed for mobile phones. One that ran across European cities had players calling in for clues and searching for the answers (much like some car rallies), which then led to more of the story and choices. A team led by Jim Schuyler, including yours truly, took this idea and elaborated on it. Jim developed an architecture that lets us develop games in which you get e-mails, voicemails, or text messages (Short Message Service, or SMS) . . . and you may respond by sending faxes, or going to a Web site, or . . . you get the idea; the game is spread out across media both in communicating to you and you communicating back to the game. Much like the movie *The Game,* we see this as a game that penetrates your life, beginning to spread the practice in larger chunks. We see this as a great avenue for certain learning activities.

Personalization

As mentioned earlier, we can use learners' performances in a game engine to adjust the difficulty of problems they face, thus creating a personalized learning experience. This is the approach of intelligent tutoring systems (ITS), an active research area using artificial intelligence to choose appropriate problems and provide guidance. They do quite a bit more, of course, understanding people's problem-solving plans and doing fine-grained analyses on learners' understanding. Eventually we hope our systems will be similarly capable, but currently such systems are very time-intensive to develop and have generally worked only in well-defined domains. There are other ways to personalize, however.

Our knowledge about individual learning styles is relatively undeveloped. Following Joe Miller's vision of exposing learners to their own characteristics as learners, I had the good fortune to lead a stellar team to develop an intelligent system that adapted the learning experience based upon individual learning characteristics. In researching what styles were out there, we realized that there were lots of models that used a few dimensions (for example, Kolb's [1981] two dimensions or Myers-Briggs with four), but there was a great deal of overlap and little coherence. Trying to make sense of it, the team ended up identifying thirty-one dimensions (!) of individual learning differences. This number suggests ample opportunity for adaptation of a game to learners.

Using learning objects at a fine granularity, we were having the objects come in different orders for different types of learners. For games, there is no reason we couldn't profile learners initially, or through their actions, and have the game engine adapt the templates not only on knowledge, but also on how the decision is presented or supported. This is, however, still a dream.

Meta-Learning

One of the most important emergent areas to focus on in learning is *meta-learning,* or learning to learn. The goal is to have people aware of how they learn and solve problems to optimize their approaches and broaden their repertoire of learning skills. The opportunity is to learn faster, better, and more. (Marcia Conner's book *Learn More Now* is a great example [Connor, 2004].) I've been working with some colleagues in the Meta-Learning Lab, and I bring this interest to learning in general and e-learning more specifically, particularly games.

One of the benefits of e-learning is the capability to keep a record of actions to reflect on or share with a mentor. Going beyond focusing on the domain, we can focus on our initial approach to a problem, our problem-solving approaches, and even our learning approaches. Another possibility is actually building meta-learning coaches into a learning environment.

We can do this with games as well. In addition to keeping records, as suggested above, we can build coaches. In the "Quest" game (Case Study 1), where kids explored a couple of small cities while trying to survive, we built in a very simple coach that watched certain simple behaviors and advised accordingly. (The idea came from work in intelligent tutoring systems.) As mentioned, we tracked the number of moves made early on versus how much area was covered, and suggested more rigorous exploration when there was too much movement without enough ground covered. To generalize, in any environment where we know the constraints and opportunities, we can build coaches that can watch for particular behaviors we want to commend or remediate.

This is an area of great opportunity in the future. We need more focus on meta-learning in general, but making it intrinsic to our environments both makes it more obvious and helps us develop our own and others' learning skills.

New Input and Output Technologies

Another area that is being explored in games is new forms of input and output (I/O). Although these I/O approaches may not yet be practical for e-learning games, there may be special applications for which they are suited, or they soon may be practical or built into devices.

One of the technologies is motor feedback. Already controllers for game consoles have vibration built in. This is a powerful channel for communication to indicate physical consequences of actions. Certainly a mobile phone with a "vibrate" option is one possibility. If you can guarantee that your learner device has this capability and you have the ability for your technical solution to influence it, you have a new channel to communicate and enhance your game. Even if it's an optional channel there may be an enhancement to the experience.

We also can read more aspects of the body. Biofeedback, through sensors attached to the body, such as the heart rate variability measure from the Institute of HeartMath's research (here's a case where galvanic skin response makes sense), can give you insight into your body's reactions and train you to foster new, more effective ones. The game "Journey to the Wild Divine" has already pioneered in this realm.

Similarly, various systems allow even severely disabled folks to control computational systems, and games have therapeutic applications. We might retrain motor skills in people with damaged nervous systems, for instance.

The physical experience is coming alive in other ways. Using joysticks as input devices can provide more direct mappings to learning tasks. We already have prototype devices that recognize how they're tilted or being moved, and we have camera recognition devices that can determine how your whole body moves.

The latter capability, movement recognition, brings in what Bill Buxton (1995) termed *haptic* input. This is gestural input that tracks hand movements and uses them as input. Particularly for training motor movements, providing feedback can allow us to train the *proprioceptive* system (the system that provides feedback about how your joints are moving, such as letting you close your eyes and touch your nose, which some argue is a sixth sense).

We're also getting virtual reality and video "caves." We can immerse the player in a full visual environment, either through a head-mounted display or surrounding them with video "walls." For certain training situations, these full-immersion visual environments have been invaluable, such as in fear minimization. These visual environments have also been used in pain minimization. Combined with gestural recognition, such visual immersion gets even more powerful, such as helping learners manipulate atoms to understand molecular bonding. We can also augment vision with heads-up displays. Just as pilots can get data overlaid on their windshield, we can start adding visual information on top of the learner's field of view through special glasses.

Voice recognition is getting remarkably good, too, as is speech generation. Just as we use voice commands on phone menus, we can use them for phone games as well. Imagine being able to play a game on the phone by speaking. We don't use audio enough in games, it has been pointed out, and sound can provide great cues. As speech recognition comes into play, we'll have some interesting opportunities for more closely mapping to real tasks.

Design Magic

Each of these technologies gives us new opportunities. Combined they can be even more powerful. Arthur C. Clarke (1984) said that any truly advanced technology is indistinguishable from magic. We can use that as a design prompt: What would we do if we had magic? That is a design rubric I used with my interaction design students, and it still has resonance. Increasingly, our limitations are not technical but of the imagination. Don't let the limits be between your ears!

9

Conclusion

A NUMBER OF YEARS AGO, I forecast that in the future there would be fun, little interactive activities that would teach us anything we wanted to learn, including how to make such fun, little interactive activities. (I think little learning activities could be a great marketing tool, by the way; marketing is, ideally, customer education. Are there any marketers who want to talk about it?) I'd like to believe that this book is a step in that direction. As Alan Kay (1971) suggested, the best way to predict the future is to create it.

Similarly, James Gilmore (2003) wrote that we have moved from an information economy to an experience economy; people are now paying to take vacations organized around themes, increasingly purchasing tickets to more complex and involving theater, and getting involved in activities that are participatory and distributed such as mobile games. His premise is that the next step is experiences that transform us—experiences that give us new capabilities, change our attitudes, and leave us thinking in new ways. That is a wonderful vision, and the principles to design such experiences are in this book.

By now I hope you believe that games are a better way of learning and that there is a systematic process to create them. To finish off, there are several things we need to do. First we need to review where we've been, then I need to help you get started, keep this knowledge active, and go further on your own.

Where We've Been

In Chapter Two we arrived at an enhanced instructional design model. This model was derived from converging elements, including previous models and research. The model focuses on cognitive skills and includes an abbreviated and dramatic introduction, multiple conceptual representations of the skill basis, cognitively annotated examples of application of the skill, scaffolded practice opportunities, and guided reflection. We also established several criteria that are essential in creating meaningful learning experiences.

Chapter Three reviewed approaches to experience design, including literature, theater, computer interface design, and, of course, games. Just as we did with learning, we extracted some common principles that defined compelling experiences.

We reviewed the elements from the two domains in Chapter Four and found that they aligned. We created a common vocabulary with which to move forward. And we detailed the components of those elements. We also reviewed a case study illustrating those principles in practice.

In Chapter Five we covered several levels of the combination of games and learning. Recognizing that not all situations warrant a full game engine, we identified mini-scenarios, linked scenarios, and contingent scenarios as approximations. These different implementations move along a grade of increasing implementation effort and consequent increasing effectiveness and engagement. We illustrated them, too, with case studies.

Chapter Six derived a design process that would provide guidance about reliably and repeatedly developing games. Starting with the basics of design, we moved through some principles to pay attention to, ending up with a proposed design process. We identified a major theme of focusing on decisions and capturing common misconceptions. We also discussed a large number of considerations to keep in mind.

We reviewed many pragmatic issues in Chapter Seven. These included the use of media, pragmatics of production, and the ever-present concerns about budget. We also talked about how audiences differ and ways to accommodate them.

Chapter Eight provided a glimpse into the future. We talked about technologies and the consequent capabilities they'd bring, as well as issues that are as yet unresolved. Although there is a lot we can do now, there will be even more interesting applications coming.

To reiterate the point of the book, we can and should make learning engaging. We do so by focusing on the decisions learners make with the knowledge and addressing common misconceptions. We have several different depths to which we can pursue this notion. We use a design process that includes learner interests and motivations, identifies a thematic world, and then systematically works to develop the details to make the story in that world compelling, focused, and manageable. Finally we test to see that we've achieved our goals and iterate until we do. That is what we've got to do; now it's time to do it.

It's not magic. There are underlying principles we can draw upon to guide us. The skills are learnable. Learning them takes understanding the elements, practicing, reflecting, all the things we talked about as effective for learning.

Just Do It

There's no time like the present to get started. I hope you've already started thinking about how you're going to use this information, that is, if you haven't already started using it. Like the learning approach advocated above, you've got the concepts and examples, now it's time for practice.

If nothing else, you should look at every learning design exercise as an opportunity to apply this approach. I'd like you to do much more, however.

When you are learning something, imagine what a game to learn it would look like. Restructure your own informal learning to be more gamelike. Use it with your kids or with others' kids. Be kidlike yourself.

You should, of course, look at anything anyone else has done. Critique it, constructively (whether you give it to them or not). We know that the practice of critiquing facilitates our ability to internalize that skill and turn it upon our own work. Again, figure out how you could turn it into a game. My claim is that there isn't a learning objective I can't make a game of (though I reserve the right to raise the level of the outcome to be knowledge application at least). See whether you can live up to that challenge.

Deal with the affect: notice whether you feel that an experience is difficult, silly, or nonobvious. Keep up your motivation by recalling that the outcome is superior to other approaches of e-learning. Think of your learners, and what would be their preference. Most important, think of what the experience should be for the learners in order to engage their minds, pull them through activities that develop their understanding, and leave them changed with new abilities and enthusiasm. Remember that thinking in terms of designing experiences, too, is an acquired skill, and it will take practice and time to make the process automatic. You'll need support, reference, and feedback. You have the responsibility to structure your own learning, but that includes bringing in help when you need it.

When faced with obstacles and doubt from others, marshal your arguments. Be firm in your conviction, be forthright about your reasons, and keep your focus on the optimum learning outcome for the optimal investment. As you've come this far, I hereby anoint you a crusader for great learning experiences and authorize you to fight the good fight. You've heard the reasons, understood the framework, adopted the design process, and seen the outcomes. Now it's time to make it happen.

Develop the component skills. Stay abreast of what people say about learning. At conferences, look for talks about the value of making learners laugh, using dramatic presentations, and keeping learners motivated. Read books, trade magazines, and journal articles—whatever you can find. Similarly, see what's being said about having fun. And, of course, have fun yourself. As mentioned before, you now have license to read novels, watch movies, and play games.

Afterwards, reflect. What made that a learning experience? How do *you* learn? What made that an engaging experience? What do *you* like? When do *you* find yourself seeking out more, and why?

Make your own learning fun. When you understand that learning is fun, you find out that you do more of it. Keep on learning and having fun!

When to Do It

One of the things I'd like to emphasize is that the earlier in a project you start thinking like this, the better. I've come in late on projects, and although there are valuable tweaks that can be done, I usually find that a major restructure would be helpful but impossible to consider at the advanced stage. I told the story in Chapter Six about a game in which a character was responsible for the novelty action (random movements forward or backward of the learner) in contrast to the character's motivation of having the learner succeed. I suggested another, thematic, grounding for these movements that did not conflict with this character's goals. The client agreed, but it was too late in the production process to regenerate the associated media.

It is premature to be able to quantify the additional value that the engaged learning approach provides. Although there are theoretical reasons and empirical research about the qualitative benefits, I don't yet know of reliable guidelines or heuristics. However, we can make a reasonable analogy from the usability field. When I worked at Access Australia Cooperative Multimedia Centre, a subsidiary was the Australian Multimedia Testing Centre (which now is the parent business). It had a quantitative model of the costs of postponing usability till late in the engineering cycle. You either got only minimal improvements to the usability (such that you still had the potential for significantly greater training and support costs, as well as lost customer loyalty) or you had major reengineering costs. I want to suggest that there are similar relationships in designing learning.

In my experience, starting with an engaged learning design approach from the beginning provides the opportunity to put reasonable costs in designing an experience up-front and is more cost effective than incurring later and larger costs in trying to make an inherently insufficient design compelling. This provides benefits by using the inherent challenge in the learning objective to make the experience engaging and effective. In the cases where focusing on engagement came in late, only minor improvements to the overall experience were possible. These were still valuable, I believe, in terms of making the experience more motivating and effective than they had been, but they were short of making the major improvement that an early focus would have provided.

So, please, go into a project with this approach, don't bring it in later. Of course, if you already have a project under way, it is better to bring this in at all rather than not, but I'd recommend you start again. (And I realize this is the real world we live in, so I will understand when you can't.)

Where to Go for Further Information

I've pointed to resources along the way, but I'd like to point you to places you should continue to monitor and new events that should be happening. Should you desire to dig deeper (and you should), there are a number of ways to do so. Resources include relevant books, people, societies, and Web sites.

Books

This is undoubtedly not the last book on the subject, as the topic has become hot. I hope it's the best one on design, as I have searched diligently and found no better framework, but there will be others that illuminate other facets of e-learning design. In addition to the ones I've already mentioned, I know of several Pfeiffer books in production that will deal with different aspects.

People

There are a number of people talking about things like making training fun, such as Sivasailam Thiagarajan, commonly known as Thiagi. There are others who come from different takes on the situation. I've generally found anyone who has recognized that there is a synergy between learning and engagement to be worth hearing, if for nothing else than inspiration, but generally the people I've heard have offered new takes on the material that illuminate facets in richer nuance than I've been able to capture here.

Societies

The most obvious relevant society is the North American Simulation and Gaming Association (NASAGA). They cover a broad range of gaming and simulation reasons, but they also have rich resources on how to develop games and simulations, and learning is a major area of their focus.

Naturally, the major training and learning societies also have a focus in this area. Both the American Society for Training and Development (ASTD) and the International Society for Performance and Improvement (ISPI) hold talks and have articles on this topic. The special focus of the e-Learning Guild makes it another natural society, and it is particularly relevant for technology-based approaches. The Emergent Learning Forum covers games and other advanced topics regularly. The Association for Educational Computing Technology (AECT) is an insightful but rather academic group.

On the computer game side, there's the Game Developers Association and the International Game Developers Association. The latter, as far as I can tell, is more thoughtful; the former, more practical (it runs a major industry conference).

Online Resources

Two major discussion groups cover learning technology issues and include games as an area of interest. I regularly read ITFORUM and IFETS (IFETS stands for International Forum for Education, Technology, and Society). The former is a more academically focused forum and has a regular schedule of paper presentations and discussions. The latter is sponsored by the IEEE (Institute of Electrical and Electronics Engineers) and has perhaps a broader reach, with the pluses and minuses that brings.

As with many hot, new areas, there are several new sites competing to be the locus in this area. The Woodrow Wilson International Center for Scholars has launched the Serious Games initiative (seriousgames.org). The Education Arcade (educationarcade.org) has been initiated by current and past students of the Games-to-Teach Project of the Comparative Media Studies department at the Massachusetts Institute of Technology.

Engaging Learning: The Site

There is a site associated with this book, engaginglearning.com, and it is my goal to keep it current with pointers to the latest and most interesting stuff.

Tally Ho!

On a personal note, I have been surprised (and thrilled) with how this book flowed while writing. Of course, I've continued to be active and have continued tweaking it (and will probably do so up until publication). The experience has been very positive, and I take that as a confirmation that the material is coherent and right, at least in my head. I hope it has made it to the page intact and that your experience has been as straightforward, inspiring, and empowering as possible (it is *hard* fun we're talking about, after all).

My goal with the book is to provide a useful guide to developing games. I have seen too much of the same old e-learning (knowledge present and knowledge test, or drill-and-kill), and knew I couldn't single-handedly make it all right. I realized that I needed a way to get more people capable and motivated and actually doing learning game design.

I hope that you feel empowered to design e-learning games, are now passionate to do so, and that you will go forth and DO so. I wish you a good trip and good luck.

Learning can, and should, be hard fun!

BIBLIOGRAPHY

Adams, E. (2004). Designing with gameplay modes and flowboards. San Francisco: Gamasutra. [http://www.gamasutra.com/features/20040510/adams_01.shtml].

Aldrich, C. (2004). *Simulations and the future of learning: An innovative (and perhaps revolutionary) approach to e-learning.* San Francisco: Pfeiffer.

Allen, M. (2002). *Michael Allen's guide to e-learning: Building interactive, fun, and effective learning programs for any company.* San Francisco: Pfeiffer.

Barrows, H. S. (1986). A taxonomy of problem-based learning methods. *Medical Education, 20*(6), 481–486.

Bloom, B. S., & Krathwohl D, R. (1956). Taxonomy of educational objectives: The classification of educational goals, by a committee of college and university examiners. *Handbook I: Cognitive domain.* New York: Longman, Green.

Brown, J. S., Collins, A., & Duguid, P. (1989). Situated cognition and the culture of learning. *Educational Researcher, 18*(1), 32–41.

Buxton, W.A.S. (1995). Touch, gesture and marking. In R. M. Baecker, J. Grudin, W.A.S. Buxton, & S. Greenberg (Eds.), *Readings in human-computer interaction: Toward the year 2000* (2nd ed.). San Francisco: Morgan Kaufman.

Campbell, J. (1972). *The hero with a thousand faces.* Princeton, NJ: Princeton University Press.

Campbell, J. (1991). *The power of myth.* New York: Anchor Books.

Carroll, J. M. (1982). The adventure of getting to know a computer. *IEEE Computer, 15*(11), 49–58.

Carroll, J. M. (1990). *The Nurnberg funnel: Designing minimalist instruction for practical computer skill.* Cambridge: MIT Press.

Chandler, P., & Sweller, J. (1991). Cognitive load theory and the format of instruction. *Cognition and Instruction, 8,* 293–332.

Clark, R. C., & Mayer, R. E. (2003). *e-Learning and the science of instruction.* San Francisco: Pfeiffer.

Clarke, A. C. (1984). *Profiles of the future: An inquiry into the limits of the possible* (Rev ed.). New York: Henry Holt & Co.

Cognition and Technology Group [at Vanderbilt]. (1990). Anchored instruction and its relationship to situated cognition. *Educational Researcher, 19*(6), 2–10.

Collins, A., Brown, J. S., & Newman, S. (1989). Cognitive apprenticeship: Teaching the craft of reading, writing, and mathematics. In L. B. Resnick (Ed.), *Knowing, learning and instruction: Essays in honor of Robert Glaser.* Mahwah, NJ: Lawrence Erlbaum.

Conner, M. L. (2004). *Learn more now: 10 simple steps to learning better, smarter, & faster.* Hoboken, NJ: Wiley.

Crawford, C. (1990). Lessons from computer game design. In B. Laurel (Ed.), *The art of human-computer interface design.* Reading, MA: Addison-Wesley.

Crawford, C. (2003). *Chris Crawford on game design.* Indianapolis: New Riders.

Csikszentmihalyi, M., & Csikszentmihalyi, I. S. (1988). *Optimal experience: Psychological studies of flow in consciousness.* New York: Cambridge University Press.

Denning, S. (2000). *The springboard: How storytelling ignites action in knowledge-era organizations.* Oxford: Butterworth Heinemann.

Freeman, D. (2004). *Creating emotion in games: The craft and art of Emotioneering*™. Indianapolis: New Riders.

Gagné, R., Briggs, L., & Wager, W. (1992). *Principles of instructional design* (4th ed.). Fort Worth, TX: HBJ College Publishers.

Gee, J. P. (2003). *What video games have to teach us about learning and literacy.* New York: Palgrave Macmillan.

Gilmore, J. H. (2003). Frontiers of the experience economy. *Batten Briefings, August 2003.* Charlottesville, VA: Darden Business Publishing.

Goldman, W. (1989). *Adventures in the screen trade.* New York: Warner.

Hogg, R. (July, 2002). Coming to terms with ICT training. *Australian Technology & Business.* [http://www.zdnet.com.au/news/business/0,39023166,20266517,00.htm].

Hutchins, E. L., Hollan, J. D., & Norman, D. A. (1986). Direct manipulation interfaces. In S. W. Draper & D. A. Norman (Eds.), *User centered system design: New perspectives on human-computer interaction.* Mahwah, NJ: Lawrence Erlbaum.

Johnson-Laird, P. N., Legrenzi, P., & Legrenzi, M. S. (1972). Reasoning and a sense of reality. *British Journal of Psychology, 10,* 64–99.

Jonassen, D. H., Howland, J., Moore, J., & Marra, R. M. (2003). *Learning to solve problems with technology: A constructivist perspective* (2nd ed.). Columbus, OH: Merrill/Prentice-Hall.

Kay, A. (1971). [http://www.smalltalk.org/alankay.html].

Keller, J. (1983). Motivational design of instruction. In Reigeluth, C. (Ed.), *Instructional-design theories and models: An overview of their current status.* Mahwah, NJ: Lawrence Erlbaum.

Kolb, D. A. (1981). Learning styles and disciplinary differences. In A. W. Chickering (ed.), *The modern American college.* San Francisco: Jossey-Bass.

Laurel, B. (1991). *Computers as theatre.* Reading, MA: Addison-Wesley.

Lave, J. (1988). *Cognition in practice: Mind, mathematics and culture in everyday life.* Cambridge, UK: Cambridge University Press.

Lepper, M. R., & Cordova, D. I. (1992). A desire to be taught: Instructional consequences of intrinsic motivation. *Motivation & Emotion, 16*(3), 187–208.

Mager, R. (1975). *Preparing instructional objectives* (2nd ed.). Belmont, CA: Lake Publishing Co.

Malone, T. W. (1981). Towards a theory of intrinsically motivating instruction. *Cognitive Science, 5,* 333–370.

McCloud, S. (1993). *Understanding comics: The invisible art.* New York: Kitchen Sink Press.

Merrill, M.D. (1983). Component display theory. In C. Reigeluth (Ed.), *Instructional design theories and models.* Mahwah, NJ: Lawrence Erlbaum.

Moser, R. (2000). *A methodology for the design of educational computer adventure games.* University of New South Wales Ph.D. thesis. [http://www.library.unsw.edu.au/~thesis/adt-NUN/public/adt-NUN20021003.141152/].

Muller, M. (1993). PICTIVE: Democratizing the dynamics of the design session. In D. Schuler & A. Namioka (Eds.), *Participatory design.* Mahwah, NJ: Lawrence Erlbaum.

Nielsen, J. (1994). Heuristic evaluation. In J. Nielsen & R. L. Mack (Eds.), *Usability inspection methods.* New York: Wiley.

Norman, D. A. (1990). *The design of everyday things.* NY: Doubleday.

Norman, D. A. (1993). *Things that make us smart.* Reading, MA: Addison-Wesley.

Norman, D. A. (2003). *Emotional design: Why we love (or hate) everyday things.* New York: Basic Books.

O'Driscoll, T. (2003). Proposing an optimal learning architecture for the digital enterprise. *Educational Technology, 43*(1), 23–119.

Prensky, M. (2000). *Digital game-based learning.* New York: McGraw-Hill Higher Education.

Reigeluth, C., & Stein, F. (1983). The elaboration theory of instruction. In C. Reigeluth (Ed.), *Instructional design theories and models.* Mahwah, NJ: Lawrence Erlbaum.

Rollings, A., & Adams, E. (2003). *Andrew Rollings and Earnest Adams on game design.* Indianapolis: New Riders.

Schank, R., & Cleary, C. (1995). *Engines for education.* Mahwah, NJ: Lawrence Erlbaum.

Shneiderman, B. (1983). Direct manipulation: A step beyond programming languages. *IEEE Computer, 16,* 57–69.

Singley, M. K., & Anderson, J. R. (1989). *The transfer of cognitive skill.* Cambridge: Harvard University Press.

Spiro, R. J., Feltovich, P. J., Jacobson, M. J., & Coulson, R. L. (1992). Cognitive flexibility, constructivism and hypertext: Random access instruction for advanced knowledge acquisition in ill-structured domains. In T. Duffy & D. Jonassen (Eds.), *Constructivism and the technology of instruction.* Mahwah, NJ: Lawrence Erlbaum.

Stephenson, N. (1996). *The diamond age, or a young girl's illustrated primer.* New York: Bantam Books.

Thiagarajan, S. (2003). *Laws of learning: 14 important principles every trainer should know.* [http://www.thiagi.com/laws-of-learning.html].

Tognazzini, B. (1993). Principles, techniques, and ethics of stage magic and their application to human interface design. *Proceedings of the International Joint Conference on Human-Computer Interaction.* Amsterdam, April.

Tufte, E. R. (1990). *Envisioning information.* Cheshire, CT: Graphics Press.

Tufte, E. R. (1997). *Visual explanations: Images and quantities, evidence and narrative.* Cheshire, CT: Graphics Press.

Tufte, E. R. (2001). *The visual display of quantitative information* (2nd ed.). Cheshire, CT: Graphics Press.

Van Merriënboer, J.J.G. (1997). *Training complex cognitive skills: A four-component instructional design model for technical training.* Englewood Cliffs, NJ: Educational Technology Publications.

Vorhaus, J. (1994). *The comic toolbox: How to be funny even if you're not.* Beverly Hills, CA: Silman-James.

Vygotsky, L. S. (1978). In M. Cole, V. John-Steiner, S. Scribner, & E. Souberman (Eds.), *Mind in society.* Cambridge: Harvard University Press.

INDEX

A

Acceptable uncertainty, and game effectiveness, 46
Adams, E., 126, 137
ADDIE design process, 123, 124–125
Affect: ARCS instructional model and, 27; as element of design, 63–64, 71, 134, 179; information processing and, 180; learning and, 12
Age, designing for, 169–170
Algorithms, use of, 147
Allen, M., 62, 125
American Society for Training and Development (ASTD), 193
Analogical reasoning, 41
Anchored instruction, 31–32
Anderson, J. R., 32
Animation: costs of, 158; versus graphics, 165
ARCS (Attention, Relevance, Confidence, & Satisfaction) model of instructional design, 27

Artificial intelligence (AI), 183–184
Audio: as dynamic media, 163–165; and speech recognition technology, 186; and use of music/noises, 165
Avatar, character development of, 141

B

Barrows, H. S., 14
Behavioral objectives, in design framework, 124
Benchmarks, game effectiveness, 46
Biofeedback, 185
Bloom, B. S., 26
Branching scenarios. *See* Contingent scenarios
Briggs, L., 26
Brown, J. S., 30, 32
Budget, and design choice, 157–159
Buxton, W.A.S., 186

C

Campbell, J., 44

Carroll, J. M., 31, 46

Cartoons and comics, 163; communication power of, 167; value and ease of using, 85–86, 166–167

Challenges: adjustment of, 139, 164; as element of engagement, 43–44, 49, 58–59, 135; incorporating into game, 67–68; and levels of play, 67

Chandler, P., 164

Clark, R. C., 164

Clarke, A. C., 186

Cleary, C., 14, 31

Coaching engine, 67–68, 184–185

Cognition and Technology Group at Vanderbilt, 14, 31

Cognitive apprenticeship model, 30–31

Cognitive flexibility theory, 31

Collins, A., 30, 32

Complexity, engaged learning and, 27, 33, 135

Component display theory, 124

Computer game design: elements of engagement in, 43–44, 46; level design concept in, 47–48; meaningful narrative in, 45

Conner, M. L., 32, 184

Console game: defined, 40–41; tutorials, 145

Constructivist learning approaches, 32

Content model, 81–82

Contingent scenarios, 142; advantages/ disadvantages of, 96; case study of, 96–102; flow diagram for, 99–101(*fig*); learners' misconceptions and, 95; tracking performance in, 174

Control, as element of engagement, 43–44, 46

Cordova, D. I., 14

Corporate e-learning strategy, 80–87

Costs: of alternatives to game engine, 158–159; media, 164; production values and, 158

Coulson, R. L., 31

Crawford, C., 47, 126

Creativity, sources of inspiration for, 138

Critiquing, value of, 190

Csikszentmihalyi, I. S., 43

Csikszentmihalyi, M., 43

Culture-specific games, 168

Curiosity, as element of engagement, 43–44

D

Decision points, tools for capturing, 147–148

Decisions, defined, 33

"Déjà Vu," 57

Denning, S., 4, 45

Design document: in gaming industry, 126; for model-based designs, 151

Design documentation, reasons for, 138–139

Design of Everyday Things, The (Norman), 145

Design teams, 116, 125; advantages of, 175; necessary skills for, 176–177; potential problems for, 175; in usability design, 175–176

Developmental level, designing for, 169–170

"Diamond Age, The," 172

Direct manipulation, in HCI studies, 46

DreamWeaver, 161

Drug therapy demo case study: feedback and outcomes, 111–112; game model for, 109–112; overview, 107–108; practice tasks in, 109; subject matter experts' role in, 111

Duguid, P., 32

E

Ease of learning, as design criterion, 117

Elaboration theory, 27

e-Learning Guild, 193

Emergent Learning Forum, 193

Emotional Design (Norman), 179–180

Emotional experience, cognition and, 12, 15

Empirical testing, 120

Engaged design: knowledge application in, 128–132; learning in context and, 129; meaningful practice in, 128–132; overview, 132–133 (*Exhibit 6.2*); secondary objectives in, 135; target performance in, 132; typical learner problems and, 130–131; usability testing in, 152–153

Engaged design model: analysis phase of, 133–136; implementation of, 146–150, 151; qualitative, set of rules in, 147–148; quantitative environment for, 147; random population of, 148–149; specification phase of, 136–151

Engaged learning: affect and, 12, 180; defined, 3; and engagement-education alignment, 2, 3(*tab*), 11, 18, 54–55(*tab*); learning theory and, 14, 15; value of, 14–15, 17–18. *See also* Learning

Engagement metrics, 152

Engaging experiences, 11–13; common elements of, 43–44, 48–49; in computer game design, 47–48; and computer interface design, 45–46; elements of drama in, 46; flow state in, 43, 46; narrative and, 44–45

Environments: programming, 104–105, 162; technology, 127, 173–174; visual, 186

Evaluation: authentic, 173; educational metrics for, 152–153; expert, 171; heuristic, 170; measures, 117; process, 121–122; scoring and success rules in, 174; statistical significance and, 121; usability, 125; and usability goals, 152; user testing as, 170–171

"EverQuest," 171

Evolutionary prototyping, 120

Experience(s): as element of engagement, 43–44; emotional, 12, 15; of flow, 43, 46; psychological aspects of, 43–44. *See also* Interface experiences; Learning experiences

Experience design field, 173

Extreme programming movement, 176

F

Facilitator guidelines, 4–5

Fantasy, engagement and, 43–44

Feedback, 46; mechanism, 57; requirements, 142; and story context, 62–63; and theme, 57

Feltovich, P. J., 31

Flash, 93, 182; full games developed in, 160

Flow diagrams, 149–150

4C/ID (four-component instructional design), 31

Freeman, D., 47, 126

Functional fixedness, as design trap, 118

G

Gagné, R., 26

Game, The (movie), 183

Game(s): commercial, as tools, 160; cultural barriers to using, 167–168; defined, 15; as evaluation environments, 173–174; major categories of, 40–43

Game design. See Learning game design

Game Developers Association, 193

Game engine model: advantages of, 142–143; case study based on, 107–112; costs of, 157–158; design teams and, 177; help and feedback in, 144; implementation requirements for, 104–105, 146; nondeterministic outcome in, 104; overview, 102–103; scenarios and, 104; simulations and, 103–105; specifications for, 105–107; success rules in, 174; tools for, 159–160; underlying model for, 102, 104, 146, 147

Game industry: compared to movie industry, 125–126; constraints in, 126; design process in, 127–128; game criteria in, 127; technology environment for, 127; testing and quality control in, 128

Game platforms, 40–41

Game play, defining elements of, 137

Gender, and game design, 58

Genre, choice of, 137

Gilmore, J. H., 187

Goal clarity, as design element, 49

Goal-based scenarios, 31

Goldman, W., 175

Graphics: versus animation, 165; conceptual, 163

Group games, 171–172

H

Haptic input, 186

Help system, 144, 147–148

High-fidelity simulations, 12

Hogg, R., 15

Hollan, J. D., 46

Howland, J., 32
HTML, uses of, 98, 158, 161
Human-computer interaction (HCI), elements of engagement in, 45–46
Humor, use of, 139, 166
Hutchins, E. L., 46
HyperCard: as development environment, 65; as prototyping tool, 159

I

IFETS, 193
Input-output interreferentiality, 49
Instructional design, 24–28; ADDIE prototypical approach to, 123–125; defined, 25; design teams and, 125; elements of learning in, 27–28; empirical basis of, 25; enhanced model of, 35(*fig*), 76–77; instruction cycle and, 25(*fig*); models, 30–33, 35; specification, 124; structure, 27–28; theoretical frameworks for, 26–27
Instructional navigation structure, component-based, 82(*fig*)
Instructional system design (ISD). *See* Instructional design
Instructional task, help system for, 144
Intelligent tutoring systems (ITS), 183–184
Interactive learning, 12; mobile devices for, 182
Interface experiences: direct options in, 70; dramatic elements in, 46
Interface(s), 158; cost factors in choosing, 158; design tools, 161; help system, 144; mapping learning to, 144–146; theme and, 56; tutorial for, 145–146; wireframe versions of, 138
International Society for Performance and Improvement (ISPI), 193
Issue-based information systems (IBIS), 139
ITFORUM, 193

J

Jacobson, M. F., 31
Job aids: creation of, 142, 143; as learning objects, 181
Johnston-Laird, P. N., 14
Jonassen, D. H., 32
"Journey to the Wild Divine," 185

K

Kay, A., 187
Keller, J., 26, 27
Knowledge application: disparate contexts for, 79; in engaged design, 128–133; learning objectives and, 33
Knowledge taxonomies, 26
Knowledge testing: versus knowledge application, 33, 128, 129(*tab*); in mini-scenarios, 78–79
Kolb, D. A., 184
Krathwohl, D. R., 26

L

Laurel, B., 46
Lave, J., 14
Learner characteristics: personalized learning and, 183–184; setting and, 137; types of, 134
Learner misconceptions: choosing distractors for, 130–131; in contingent scenarios, 95; story-based feedback on, 134
Learner styles, support for, 82
Learning: cycle, 24(*fig*); cognitive research on, 30–33; goals, 29–30, 116; as "hard fun," 10; hierarchy of knowledge in, 16–17; online, 12, 15–16; reflection and, 24, 30; retention, 29–30, scaffolded, 30; self-directed, 13; transfer, 29–30, 32. *See also* Engaged learning
Learning by doing, and game effectiveness, 46
Learning content design, 26
Learning design model: basic (waterfall), 114; five levels of, 76; implementation requirements of, 146–150; trade-offs in choice of, 112. *See also specific model*
Learning evaluation. *See* Evaluation
Learning experiences: core elements of, 27–28, 36–37, 53–55; designing, 136–139; engagement and, 4, 11–13, 39–40; and use context, 135
Learning game design: action-domain link in, 59–60, 68–69; active decision making in, 61, 69–70; adding constraints to, 119; affective elements in, 63–64, 71; brainstorming in, 118, 119; character

development in, 141; coaching tool in, 67–68, 184–185; cognitive challenge in, 58–59, 60; component stages of, 116–123; data collection and analysis in, 116–117; design traps in, 118; direct versus indirect mapping in, 61–62; element of unpredictability in, 63–64; evaluation in, 117, 121–122; feedback and help system in, 57, 62–63, 71, 130, 139, 144; future research and, 179–188; genre choice in, 59–60, 137; goals and objectives in, 10, 57, 117; implementation phase of, 120–121; incorporating difficulty levels into, 143; introduction in, 57; iterative design cycle in, 114, 115(*fig*), 117, 122–123; iterative testing in, 120; larger learning process and, 143; launching system for, 173–174; learning support in, 142–144; mapping learning to interface in, 144–146; media use in, 140; pedagogical support in, 142–144; problem-learner link in, 60, 69; process, 114–122; question set in, 120; setting in, 60; solution criteria in, 117, 118; specification process in, 118–120; spiral model of, 115; story/story line in, 56, 139–141; tutorials in, 145–146. *See also* Engaged design
Learning game design checklist, 153–154(*Exhibit 6-4*)
Learning Management System (LMS), 93, 173
Learning models: cognitive apprenticeship, 30–31; cognitive flexibility theory and, 31; constructivist, 32; convergent framework for, 27–28, 33–37; four component instructional design (4C/ID), 31; goal-based scenarios, 31; situated learning, 32; whole-body learning, 32; ZOPD (zones of proximal development), 32–33
Learning objective: cognitive development as, 58–59; defined, 3; complexity in, 33; defined, 3; and directness of transfer, 137; engaged learning approach to, 16, 18–19; establishment of, 27, 28, 34; and game design, 18–19; and knowledge application, 33; and learning-doing continuum, 15–17; and performance outcomes, 27; usability of, 133–135
Learning objects, 184; concept of, 180–181; standards, argument for, 181
Learning styles, and personalized learning experiences, 183–184
Learning technology, standards for, 180
Legrenzi, M. S. and P., 14
Lepper, J., 14, 43
Linked scenarios: case study of, 89–94; overarching story line in, 87–88; overview of, 87–89
Live training games, 172–173
Lookup table, 147–148

M

Mager, R., 26, 27
Malone, T. W., 43
Mapping: direct versus indirect, 61–62; learning to interface, 144–146
Marra, R. M., 32
Mayer, R. E., 164
McCloud, S., 167
Media: and cognitive processing capacity, 164; costs, 164; dynamic, 163, 164–165; properties, 162, 163(*tab*); roles, 162–164; theme and, 140
Media skills development (case study): design process in, 80–86; overview, 80–81; outcomes, 86–87
Merrill, M. D., 26, 124
Meta-learning, 13, 184–185
Metrics of engagement, 152
Minimalist instruction model, 31
Mini-scenarios: case study utilizing, 80–87; creating contexts in, 77–79; feedback in, 130; implementation of, 146; practice elements in, 77–79; scoring in, 174; story line in, 78–79
MMOGs (massively multiplayer online games), 171
Mobile devices for learning 182–183
Monitoring skills, 4
Moore, J., 32
Moser, R., 63, 161
Motor feedback technology, 185
Movement recognition capability, 186
Muller, M., 161

Multiplayer games: learning potential of, 171; main types of, 171; pragmatic considerations in, 172
"Myst," 159

N
Narrative: as element of engagement, 44–45; in game play, 44–45; linear, 56
Newman, S., 30
Nielsen, J., 170
Norman, D. A., 15, 46, 112, 145, 179
North American Gaming and Simulation Association (NASAGA), 193
Novelty, engagement and, 49, 79, 139, 149

O
O'Driscoll, T., 16
Online learning, drop-out rates for, 12, 15–16

P
Panda 3D, 160
Performance measures, 117
Personal digital assistant (PDA), 93
Personalized learning experience, creation of, 180–181, 183–184
Physical experience, new technologies for, 185–186
Pictive technique, 161
Pinball Construction Set, 46
Plot elements, design theme and, 56
Portfolios of performance, 174
PowerPoint application, as prototyping tool, 161
Practice tasks: creating scenarios from, 78; development of, 83–84; scaffolded, 30, 34, 83
Programming environments, 104–105; early development of, 162
"Project Management for Non–Project Managers" game, 160; challenge in, 135; design process in, 91–93; implementation of, 146; interface actions/mapping in, 146; linked scenario model for, 89–94; outcomes, 94; story line in, 92–93
Prototype: evolutionary, 120; specification, 150; tools for creating, 160–162
Pseudo-code, 147

Q
"Quest for Independence" game, 64–74; challenge in, 67; coaching engine in, 67–68, 184; context and design process, 64–65; elements of engaged learning in, 65–72; feedback in, 144; learning goals in, 67; secondary objectives in, 135; testing outcomes of, 72–74

R
Randomness: as element of engagement, 49; introduction of, 148–149; and non-deterministic outcome, 104
Reciprocal teaching, 4
Reference library, 142
Reflection, learning and, 30, 34, 35(*fig*)
Reigeluth, C., 26, 27
Relevance, as design element, 49
Resources, 192–194; game developers as, 47–48; online, 193–194
Responsiveness, as element of engagement, 46
Rollings, A., 126

S
Safe conduct, and game effectiveness, 46
Scaffolded practice, 30, 34, 35(*fig*), 83
Scenario(s): as design choice, 158–159; games and, 104; scoring in, 174. *See also* Contingent scenarios; Linked scenarios; Mini-scenarios
Schank, R., 14, 31
SCORM (Standard Content Object Reference Model), 173
Seely, J., 30
Self-directed learning, 13
Serious Games Initiative, 194
Set effects, as design trap, 118
Set of rules, 147, 149
Setting: appropriateness of, 60; and learner characteristics, 137; in mini-scenarios, 79
Shneiderman, B., 46
Simulations: defined, 15; engine-driven, 158; high-fidelity, learning in, 12; as scenario, 103
Singley, M. K., 32
Situated learning, 32
Sound effects, 140, 165

Specification: experience design and, 136–139; output of, 150–151; and participatory design approach, 176; process, 118–120; of prototype, 150
Speech generation, 186
Spiro, R. J., 31
Squeak (tool), 159
State (flow) diagrams, 149–150
Stein, F., 26, 27
Stephenson, N., 172
Story: choice of, 59–60; as context for feedback, 62–63; design theme and, 56
Story arc, 44, 45(*fig*)
Story board: creation of, 138, 141, 151; linear, sample of, 92–93
Story line: branching, 97, 98; coherence in, 140–141; and concept presentation, 93; development and elaboration of, 139–140; embedded misconceptions in, 141; in linked scenarios, 87–89; in mini-scenario, 78–79
Subject matter experts (SMEs), 125, 131; audience as, 176
Sweller, J., 164

T

Technologies: input and output (I/O), 185–186; learning, standards for, 180; low- versus high-fidelity implementation of, 121
Technology environments, 173–174
Testing methods, 120
Theme: coherence of, 48; criteria for choosing, 60; emotionality and, 44–45; example of, 65–66; interactivity in, 56; linked to goal, 57; media and, 140; transfer and, 137; world model for, 102
Therapeutic applications, 185
Thiagarajan, S., 172
3D games, 160
Tognazzini, B., 46

Tools: as game development environment, 159, 160; implementation, 147–150; modifications of games as, 160; presentation, 161; professional, 160; prototyping, 159; simple, 158; types of, 159
Tufte, E. R., 145
Tuning process, 162
Tutorials, built into games, 145–146

U

Underengineering movement, 176
Usability design, participatory, 175–176
Usability evaluation: and learning evaluation, 125; metrics, testing and refining, 152–153; and usability goals, 152; usability-HCI field and, 122, 170
User experience, as design criterion, 117

V

Van Merriëboer, J.J.G., 14, 31, 79
Vehicle selling case study: contingent scenario created for, 96–102; design process in, 97–98; outcomes, 102
Visual Basic, 159
Visual environments, technologies for, 186
Voice recognition, 186
Vygotsky, L. S., 32

W

Wager, W., 26
Web page, appropriate composition of, 182
Whole-body learning, 32
Wire frames, defined, 138
World model, 102
Writing: contingent scenarios, 96; professionalism in, 85, 165

Z

Zone of proximal development (ZOPD), 32–33

CLARK N. QUINN is passionate about thinking and learning and is fascinated with the potential for technology to facilitate them. With a particular focus on learning systems, he has designed and developed innovative solutions for community agencies, schools, industry, and government. Clark has a special interest in making interactions engaging and has created award-winning online content, educational computer games, and more. Previously he led research and development as director of cognitive systems for Knowledge Universe Interactive Studio, and held executive positions at Open Net and Access CMC, two Australian initiatives in Internet-based multimedia and education. Clark is a recognized scholar with an extensive publication and presentation record and has held positions at the University of New South Wales, the University of Pittsburgh's Learning Research and Development Center, and San Diego State University's Center for Research in Mathematics and Science Education. Clark earned a Ph.D. in cognitive psychology from the University of California, San Diego, after working for DesignWare, an early educational game software company. Clark currently works through Quinnovation.

Pfeiffer Publications Guide

This guide is designed to familiarize you with the various types of Pfeiffer publications. The formats section describes the various types of products that we publish; the methodologies section describes the many different ways that content might be provided within a product. We also provide a list of the topic areas in which we publish.

FORMATS

In addition to its extensive book-publishing program, Pfeiffer offers content in an array of formats, from fieldbooks for the practitioner to complete, ready-to-use training packages that support group learning.

FIELDBOOK Designed to provide information and guidance to practitioners in the midst of action. Most fieldbooks are companions to another, sometimes earlier, work, from which its ideas are derived; the fieldbook makes practical what was theoretical in the original text. Fieldbooks can certainly be read from cover to cover. More likely, though, you'll find yourself bouncing around following a particular theme, or dipping in as the mood, and the situation, dictate.

HANDBOOK A contributed volume of work on a single topic, comprising an eclectic mix of ideas, case studies, and best practices sourced by practitioners and experts in the field.

An editor or team of editors usually is appointed to seek out contributors and to evaluate content for relevance to the topic. Think of a handbook not as a ready-to-eat meal, but as a cookbook of ingredients that enables you to create the most fitting experience for the occasion.

RESOURCE Materials designed to support group learning. They come in many forms: a complete, ready-to-use exercise (such as a game); a comprehensive resource on one topic (such as conflict management) containing a variety of methods and approaches; or a collection of like-minded activities (such as icebreakers) on multiple subjects and situations.

TRAINING PACKAGE An entire, ready-to-use learning program that focuses on a particular topic or skill. All packages comprise a guide for the facilitator/trainer and a workbook for the participants. Some packages are supported with additional media—such as video—or learning aids, instruments, or other devices to help participants understand concepts or practice and develop skills.

- *Facilitator/trainer's guide* Contains an introduction to the program, advice on how to organize and facilitate the learning event, and step-by-step instructor notes. The guide also contains copies of presentation materials—handouts, presentations, and overhead designs, for example—used in the program.

- *Participant's workbook* Contains exercises and reading materials that support the learning goal and serves as a valuable reference and support guide for participants in the weeks and months that follow the learning event. Typically, each participant will require his or her own workbook.

ELECTRONIC CD-ROMs and Web-based products transform static Pfeiffer content into dynamic, interactive experiences. Designed to take advantage of the searchability, automation, and ease-of-use that technology provides, our e-products bring convenience and immediate accessibility to your workspace.

METHODOLOGIES

CASE STUDY A presentation, in narrative form, of an actual event that has occurred inside an organization. Case studies are not prescriptive, nor are they used to prove a point; they are designed to develop critical analysis and decision-making skills. A case study has a specific time frame, specifies a sequence of events, is narrative in structure, and contains a plot structure—an issue (what should be/have been done?). Use case studies when the goal is to enable participants to apply previously learned theories to the circumstances in the case, decide what is pertinent, identify the real issues, decide what should have been done, and develop a plan of action.

ENERGIZER A short activity that develops readiness for the next session or learning event. Energizers are most commonly used after a break or lunch to stimulate or refocus the group. Many involve some form of physical activity, so they are a useful way to counter post-lunch lethargy. Other uses include transitioning from one topic to another, where "mental" distancing is important.

EXPERIENTIAL LEARNING ACTIVITY (ELA) A facilitator-led intervention that moves participants through the learning cycle from experience to application (also known as a Structured Experience). ELAs are carefully thought-out designs in which there is a definite learning purpose and intended outcome. Each step—everything that participants do during the activity—facilitates the accomplishment of the stated goal. Each ELA includes complete instructions for facilitating the intervention and a clear statement of goals, suggested group size and timing, materials required, an explanation of the process, and, where appropriate, possible variations to the activity. (For more detail on Experiential Learning Activities, see the Introduction to the *Reference Guide to Handbooks and Annuals*, 1999 edition, Pfeiffer, San Francisco.)

GAME A group activity that has the purpose of fostering team spirit and togetherness in addition to the achievement of a pre-stated goal. Usually contrived—undertaking a desert expedition, for example—this type of learning method offers an engaging means for participants to demonstrate and practice business and interpersonal skills. Games are effective for team building and personal development mainly because the goal is subordinate to the process—the means through which participants reach decisions, collaborate, communicate, and generate trust and understanding. Games often engage teams in "friendly" competition.

ICEBREAKER A (usually) short activity designed to help participants overcome initial anxiety in a training session and/or to acquaint the participants with one another. An icebreaker can be a fun activity or can be tied to specific topics or training goals. While a useful tool in itself, the icebreaker comes into its own in situations where tension or resistance exists within a group.

INSTRUMENT A device used to assess, appraise, evaluate, describe, classify, and summarize various aspects of human behavior. The term used to describe an instrument depends primarily on its format and purpose. These terms include survey, questionnaire, inventory, diagnostic, survey, and poll. Some uses of instruments include providing instrumental feedback to group members, studying here-and-now processes or functioning within a group, manipulating group composition, and evaluating outcomes of training and other interventions.

Instruments are popular in the training and HR field because, in general, more growth can occur if an individual is provided with a method for focusing specifically on his or her own behavior. Instruments also are used to obtain information that will serve as a basis for change and to assist in workforce planning efforts.

Paper-and-pencil tests still dominate the instrument landscape with a typical package comprising a facilitator's guide, which offers advice on administering the instrument and interpreting the collected data, and an initial set of instruments. Additional instruments are available separately. Pfeiffer, though, is investing heavily in e-instruments. Electronic instrumentation provides effortless distribution and, for larger groups particularly, offers advantages over paper-and-pencil tests in the time it takes to analyze data and provide feedback.

LECTURETTE A short talk that provides an explanation of a principle, model, or process that is pertinent to the participants' current learning needs. A lecturette is intended to establish a common language bond between the trainer and the participants by providing a mutual frame of reference. Use a lecturette as an introduction to a group activity or event, as an interjection during an event, or as a handout.

MODEL A graphic depiction of a system or process and the relationship among its elements. Models provide a frame of reference and something more tangible, and more easily remembered, than a verbal explanation. They also give participants something to "go on," enabling them to track their own progress as they experience the dynamics, processes, and relationships being depicted in the model.

ROLE PLAY A technique in which people assume a role in a situation/scenario: a customer service rep in an angry-customer exchange, for example. The way in which the role is approached is then discussed and feedback is offered. The role play is often repeated using a different approach and/or incorporating changes made based on feedback received. In other words, role playing is a spontaneous interaction involving realistic behavior under artificial (and safe) conditions.

SIMULATION A methodology for understanding the interrelationships among components of a system or process. Simulations differ from games in that they test or use a model that depicts or mirrors some aspect of reality in form, if not necessarily in content. Learning occurs by studying the effects of change on one or more factors of the model. Simulations are commonly used to test hypotheses about what happens in a system—often referred to as "what if?" analysis—or to examine best-case/worst-case scenarios.

THEORY A presentation of an idea from a conjectural perspective. Theories are useful because they encourage us to examine behavior and phenomena through a different lens.

TOPICS

The twin goals of providing effective and practical solutions for workforce training and organization development and meeting the educational needs of training and human resource professionals shape Pfeiffer's publishing program. Core topics include the following:

Leadership & Management

Communication & Presentation

Coaching & Mentoring

Training & Development

e-Learning

Teams & Collaboration

OD & Strategic Planning

Human Resources

Consulting